Presented To:

From:

Date:

RAISING A MODERN FRONTIER BOY

Directing a Film and a Life with My Son

JOHN GROOTERS
with JEDIDIAH GROOTERS

© Copyright 2012–John Grooters

All rights reserved. This book is protected by the copyright laws of the United States of America. This book may not be copied or reprinted for commercial gain or profit. The use of short quotations or occasional page copying for personal or group study is permitted and encouraged. Permission will be granted upon request. Unless otherwise identified, Scripture quotations are taken from the HOLY BIBLE, NEW INTERNATIONAL VERSION®, Copyright © 1973, 1978, 1984 International Bible Society. Used by permission of Zondervan. All rights reserved. Scripture quotations marked NKJV are taken from the New King James Version. Copyright © 1982 by Thomas Nelson, Inc. Used by permission. All rights reserved. Scripture quotations marked NASB are taken from the NEW AMERICAN STANDARD BIBLE®, Copyright © 1960,1962,1963,1968,1971,1972,1973,1975,1977,1995 by The Lockman Foundation. Used by permission. Scripture quotations marked HCSB are taken from the Holman Christian Standard Bible Copyright © 1999, 2000, 2002, 2003 by Holman Bible Publishers, Nashville Tennessee. All rights reserved. Scripture quotations marked TNIV are taken from Today's New International Version, © Copyright 2001, 2005 by Biblica. All rights reserved.

DESTINY IMAGE® PUBLISHERS, INC.
P.O. Box 310, Shippensburg, PA 17257-0310
"Promoting Inspired Lives."

This book and all other Destiny Image, Revival Press, MercyPlace, Fresh Bread, Destiny Image Fiction, and Treasure House books are available at Christian bookstores and distributors worldwide.

For a U.S. bookstore nearest you, call 1-800-722-6774.
For more information on foreign distributors, call 717-532-3040.
Reach us on the Internet: www.destinyimage.com.

ISBN 13 TP: 978-0-7684-4113-0

For Worldwide Distribution, Printed in the U.S.A.
1 2 3 4 5 6 7 8 / 16 15 14 13 12

DEDICATION

for Larry Grooters—

a much-loved pastor to many,

a wonderful Dad to me,

a rock solid BePaw to Jed,

and the original #44 in our family.

ACKNOWLEDGMENTS

My dad played basketball in high school—South High, Grand Rapids, Michigan—in the 1950s. He was number forty-four. Ever since I saw the old black and white photos of my dad shooting his patented turnaround, high-hands jump shot, forty-four was my favorite number. That's what happens when your dad is your hero. You want to be like him. You want to wear his number.

My son, Jed, whom this book is written about and with, also wore number four or forty-four on most of his jerseys growing up. I expect I'll be rooting for a grandchild one day who is sporting a four.

That's what legacy is. It's living life with such character and honor that those who come after want to emulate the values that came before. So I want to acknowledge my dad, Larry Grooters, for being a Frontier Boy father for me and an awesome grandfather to Jed.

There are so many others along the way who have made invaluable contributions to my journey as a father. I want especially to thank Bruce and Beth Snoap, Kevin and Sherry Harney, Phil and Jan McDonald, Mark DeVries, Trent and Lyn Walker, Herb Barbutti, Ray VanderLaan, John and Kathy Wright, Kevin and Michelle Holt, Terry Cutter, Leonard and Shay Hoffman, James and Andrea Karsten, Elsa Prince Broekhuizen, Mickey and Larry Grooters, and Jeff and Karen Barker. If I could, I'd thank every teacher, coach, sitter, and leader who invested integrity into Jed and modeled true manhood. We all need each other to be there for our kids. Boys need to see grown men who are actually living out the faith and values that we keep pointing toward.

I would also like to thank Joel Nori, Birch Blair, and the great team at Destiny Image for believing in *The Frontier Boys* and helping to launch both the film and this book.

Finally, I have no illusions that without a mother like Judy and a sister like Jordyn, Jed's life would have run aground a thousand times—and mine as well. Jordyn (who as of this writing is preparing for her own first-time journey of parenthood), you helped to craft your younger brother into a man of faith. That is lasting fruit. And of course, you also helped tremendously by editing Jed's sections of each chapter. Judy, my partner in everything, your story on being a mother would take a much longer book than this to capture. You are the bedrock of this family and your wisdom and insight are the foundation of this whole journey. Plus, you were the one who technically gave birth to the boy. Technically.

CONTENTS

	Foreword *by Don Cousins* 11
	Introduction 15
Chapter 1	Defining Moments 21
Chapter 2	Backstory 45
Chapter 3	Competitive Edge 59
Chapter 4	It's Up to You to Teach Him 73
Chapter 5	Sharing the Load 93
Chapter 6	Stepping into the Waters 109
Chapter 7	Partnership 125
Chapter 8	Behind the Scenes 137
Chapter 9	Make It Real 155
Chapter 10	A Thousand Generations 165

FOREWORD

By Don Cousins
Author of *Experiencing LeaderShift* and
Unexplainable, a founding pastor of
Willow Creek Church

I opened our local paper one morning a few years back and took a quick glance at the front page, as I typically do, before turning to the sports page, where my true interest lies. On this particular morning, unlike most days, I stuck with the front page as I read a headline about a high school senior who was not being permitted to read his planned speech at graduation. As I read, I soon learned why not…he was intending to read a passage from the Bible and this was simply not acceptable to school officials. I chuckled a bit, as I thought, "Their attempt to silence will only result in a louder voice." The truth of this thought was now evident as I was reading about him, his speech, and the passage (1 Cor. 10) on the front page of our only local paper.

I didn't know Jed Grooters or his family at the time. Our family was still relatively new to the community, we lived on the opposite side of town, and our kids attended a different school. Were it not for the school officials' attempt to silence Jed, it is likely that I would have never heard of this matter. Now as I read, I was encouraged to learn of a young man who was respectfully refusing to alter his speech, and more importantly, refusing to downplay his convictions concerning his faith in Jesus Christ. Thousands more in our community would also learn of this senior's convictions as they too read his now front-page story.

A few years later, I met John and Judy Grooters, Jed Grooters' parents, as their production company was helping me with a video project for a book I had written. It didn't take me long to see why their son Jed was who he was. "These people," I thought to myself, "are the real deal." They aren't merely giving lip service to following Jesus; they are truly following. Faith isn't a religious concept to them; it's a way of life that is evident in their priorities, their relationships, their family, and their business.

My video project was completed some time ago, but my relationship with the Grooters continues to this day. John and I soon learned that we had much in common, including our desire to raise sons who prove to be the "real deal" when it comes to following Jesus. We agreed that no amount of achievement in life would mean anything if our boys decided that they wanted to do life without Jesus leading the way. By God's grace, Jed, and my sons Kyle and Kirk, have chosen to place Jesus both as the foundation and at the center of their respective lives. To all three of them, faith in Jesus is not a religious concept; it is, in reality, a way of life.

If you have a son and you desire to raise him to know, love, and follow Jesus, then I strongly encourage you to read this book that you hold in your hand. In the world in which we live today, there are few assignments that present a greater challenge than that of raising kids who are the real deal for Jesus. I encourage you to get on your knees before God on behalf of your kids. I encourage you to let the Word of God serve as your instruction book for life. I encourage you to build relationships with other dads who are trying to raise sons who are the real deal for Jesus. And I encourage you to listen to those who have gone before you in this desire and have something to say out of their experience. John Grooters is one of these people. I can say with firsthand knowledge, "John is the real deal for Jesus." And one of the places where this can be most clearly seen is in the life of his son, Jed.

About a year ago, my sons, Kyle and Kirk, came across a t-shirt that caught their eye. Across the chest, it read, "Real Men Love Jesus." Our spouses, our churches, our communities, and our sons and daughters especially, are in desperate need of "real men who love Jesus." To be such a man and to raise such a man is among the greatest achievements in all of life.

By the way, some 2,000 years ago, the Roman government sought to silence a man whose testimony about Jesus was causing quite a stir. His name was Paul. Government officials decided that the best way to silence him was to throw him in prison. It was from that prison that he penned four major letters now found in the New Testament. In one of those letters, he wrote the following:

> *Now I want you to know, brethren, that my circumstances have turned out for the greater progress of the gospel, so that my imprisonment in the cause of Christ has become well known throughout the whole praetorian guard and to everyone else, and that most of the brethren, trusting in the Lord because of my imprisonment, have far more courage to speak the word of God without fear* (Philippians 1:12-14 NASB).

God used the attempt to silence Paul as a means of giving him an even louder voice. God provided Paul with access to the very heart of the Roman government (praetorian guard). In addition, many others were encouraged by his courage.

I remember that day when I read Jed's front-page story. Although I didn't know him at that time, his convictions encouraged me in mine. A brief reading, in a short speech, to a few thousand people, had now become a big deal, on the front page of the newspaper, where tens of thousands would learn of it. Who knows what God may do through a life of a young man with the courage of his convictions. May God grant us fathers with the strength and the wisdom we need to raise up sons to be such men.

INTRODUCTION

Are you a father?

Do you have a son?

If you do, then you have a job that is as important as any other job you will ever have in your life. Our world needs strong, well-adjusted men of faith now and in the coming generation. It is upon the shoulders of this generation of fathers to raise those kinds of men. Your sons are going to mature and develop based on the choices you make, on how you raise them.

I became a father before I really took the time to carefully consider the implications. Even though I had a job and a great wife, the truth is that I, like all of my peers, had no formal training in the art of parenting. I hadn't read any fatherhood books or gone to any parenting classes. Other than my own father, I didn't have any mentors.

But that was twenty-two years ago, and now that I've been down the road and back I'm happy to be a humble mentor to any guy who is embarking on this fatherhood journey. This is not a self-help book written by a certified psychologist or even a self-appointed expert in parenting. I don't counsel kids or talk on the radio. It is a book about the story of one dad and one son who worked it out together. When my son turned nineteen years old, we worked together on a faith-based feature film, "The Frontier Boys." Jed was a lead actor; I was the director. One day on the set of that film it struck me that we had made it. The son I had been raising, mentoring, and praying for had become a man fully capable of taking on life, and he held tight to a living faith in God. He had become a strong and solid man. How did it happen? Was it purely by the grace of God, or was it because of good choices made by his mother and me? The answer, of course, is some of both. This book will give you a peek behind the curtain of our story, one father and one son who have truly enjoyed the ride together. I pray that you will find encouragement and practical advice in this story as you set out to raise your own modern frontier boy, one who is ready and equipped to take on the unknown challenges of the future with courage and faith.

THE FRONTIER OF MANHOOD

Where are the modern frontiers? Where are the great unknown territories of today—the places full of promise and adventure that await the bold and the brave? Two hundred years ago, American settlers, mostly immigrants themselves, found their frontier west of the Mississippi River. For them, the frontier was a geographic reality that represented magnificent possibilities but also promised inevitable hardships. Pioneers set off for unknown and uncharted territories without cell phones, ATM cards, or GPS. They couldn't possibly know what to expect; yet, they went ahead anyway.

In our world, there isn't one square mile on the planet where one can simply plant a stake in the ground and lay claim to the land. Those geographic frontiers are long gone. But we still gaze into unknown and uncharted territory and decide whether or not it is worth the risk to go forward. We still have our frontiers. *Anything* we face where we cannot know the challenges or opportunities before us is a modern frontier. For these frontiers we are never fully prepared. How can anyone prepare for the frontiers of life? If you knew what was coming, it wouldn't be a frontier—it would be a routine.

Fatherhood is a frontier. It often comes upon you before you think you are ready, and it is fraught with magnificent possibilities and inevitable hardships. I've been there. I'm on the way home, symbolically heading back east. I imagine passing the next generation of men who are standing under the St. Louis arch ready to head west. This is the story of my journey, a simple tour guide for other men who are just setting out.

Raising a child, and particularly a boy, in today's world is a daunting challenge. Today, even the distinction of fatherhood is coming under new scrutiny and review. In some circles, it is no longer appropriate to discuss specific roles for father and mother. U.S. passport applications have replaced the designations of father and mother with the option "parent one and parent two." It can be a confusing time for any prospective father. But I believe that the father has a specific calling and responsibility. Your son will have no trouble distinguishing between his mother and his father. He needs his mother, no question, but he needs a father more than ever. Why?

For one thing, fathers are disappearing. In the United States, somewhere between one third and one half of all kids are being raised in single-parent households, and 84 percent of those households are led by the mother.[1] Millions of kids never say the word *dad* at home at all. What happens to the stability or productivity of a culture that raises half of its boys without their fathers? If you are a single dad raising boys on your own, then you have an even greater responsibility without the balance of a woman to help raise the children. You can still raise a modern frontier boy—a boy who is ready and equipped to take on the unknown challenges of the future with courage and faith—but you need to be incredibly intentional about how you raise your boys.

I am convinced that there is a specific, God-ordained role that a man should play in his son or daughter's life. It is distinct and complementary to the role a woman should play in the raising of a child. And if you are a man who has been given the privilege and responsibility of raising a child in this world, then I hope and pray this book is a help to you. If that is you, then you have been promoted to the most honorable position you will ever earn in your entire lifetime—the role of dad. You are the only person in the whole world who has the opportunity to infuse your children with the lifelong *certainty* that their earthly father loves them. My daughter, now twenty-two years old, sent me a card just last week. She said, "Do you know that I have never in my whole life had to wonder if my dad loved me? It's true. And I don't know if there are many daughters who are as blessed as I am to say that." May that be true for you as well—may there never be a day where your kids have the slightest doubt that they are loved by their fathers. It's basic and foundational. If you never knew that your father loved you, then you know the uncertainty with which you faced your future.

Another book, someday, will focus on the sacred trust between daughters and fathers. My daughter has been an unbelievable joy in my life. But on these pages I'm going to focus on sons and fathers. This is a story of one man, one boy, and their life together that led to their producing a feature film together. It's a cool story.

WHEN DOES A BOY BECOME A MAN?

In mainstream western culture we don't typically have a celebration for the rite of passage between boyhood and manhood. At age sixteen an American boy can get his driver's license; at eighteen he can vote; at twenty-one, he can legally drink a beer. That's what we have. Those might be cultural rights of passage, but they have little to do with the responsibilities and expectations of manhood. Dan Kiley, in his book *Peter Pan Syndrome: Men Who Have Never Grown Up*, reveals that many men *never* walk that passage from adolescence into adult relationships and responsibilities. Like Peter Pan, they are stuck in childhood. This is bad. This is not what we want for our sons.

I was filming a television special near Window Rock, Arizona, and spent a week with the Navajo. We shot a re-creation of a traditional Navajo Kinaalda ceremony—a rite of passage celebration for Navajo girls who experience their first period. It is a memorable and meaningful ritual for Navajo girls, and it helps them recognize and respect the changes they are going through physically and emotionally.

In Orthodox Judaism, the rite of passage ceremonies are the Bar Mitzvah and Bat Mitzvah, symbolizing the time in the life of boys and girls when, after weeks of study and guidance, they become responsible for their own adherence to the Torah.

But in my culture such rites of passage—and the opportunity for the support, understanding, and celebration that come with them—are completely missing. Boys don't know when they stand on the frontier of manhood or how they are supposed to cross into it. I can vividly remember being that age, desperately searching for handles to hold on to as I went from boyhood to adolescence to manhood. As a dad I've had a second chance to observe that transition. When did my son grow from boy to adolescent to man? How did I or could I have helped him along the way? For my son, Jed, the first big, visible, tangible leap came at the time of one rite of passage that we do celebrate in our culture—high school graduation.

NOTE

1. Timothy S. Grall, "Custodial Mothers and Fathers and Their Child Support: 2007," Issued November 2009, U.S. Department of Commerce, Economics and Statistics Administration, U.S. Census Bureau, accessed May 22, 2012, http://www.census.gov/prod/2009pubs/p60-237.pdf. Approximately 84 percent of custodial parents are mothers.

CHAPTER 1
DEFINING MOMENTS

*Principle #1: Declare your allegiances publicly;
your kids are watching.*

It began with a phone call.

"Hello, this is Kent Henson. I'm the principal at West Ottawa High School."

"Um, yes, hello." *Why is he calling us?* I wondered.

"Have you read your son's graduation speech?"

"No," I said.

"Do you think you and your wife could stop by the office this afternoon?"

This was odd. In all Jed's years in school—elementary, middle, and high school—we had never once received a call from the school principal. Jed was a no-trouble kid. He carried a 4.0 GPA, took advanced placement classes, and had been awarded the "Coach's Award" from his hockey, baseball, and tennis coaches his senior year. Everyone liked Jed—his classmates, his teachers, his teammates, and his coaches.

Jed had earned a perfect grade point, and as one of his school's valedictorians was expected to give a two-minute speech at the graduation ceremony. Each of the class valedictorians had met to rehearse their speeches aloud to one another and to the faculty advisor. Apparently there was a problem with Jed's speech. I actually wondered if the problem was that he hadn't written one.

So my wife and I drove across town to the high school. West Ottawa High School is a large school, fourth largest in Michigan, with a brand-new building and all the luxuries of modern American secondary education. Two years earlier, Jed's big sister, Jordyn, had also been honored as valedictorian of her class. The Grooters kids had done pretty well at ol' West Ottawa, and I figured that should make my wife and me honored parents around there. We were full of curiosity as we walked into the wide sky-lit corridors on a June afternoon. I had no idea what Jed had in mind for his speech. He hadn't shown me anything, and we hadn't talked about it. I didn't sense that he was particularly nervous or concerned about it. Jed is naturally easygoing, and, after all, it was only a two-minute speech.

Jed and his sister drove to the school and met us in the freshly painted office of the high school principal, Mr. Henson. We sat down in plastic chairs around a round table under harsh florescent lights. As I sat down, I began having flashbacks to my own freshman year of high school when I was occasionally summoned to the principal's office. I didn't like it then, and I didn't much like it now.

"Mr. Grooters, have you seen this?" Mr. Henson asked as he handed me a copy of Jed's speech.

"No," I answered honestly.

"Well, take a look."

I looked at the paper. I could immediately tell that Jed hadn't written this—it was blatant plagiarism! I recognized the words of the Apostle Paul as they had been published in a letter to a Greek church at Corinth. Jed was quoting from First Corinthians 10, verses 1-13. He was using Eugene Peterson's paraphrase called *The Message*. I was impressed.

Jed's speech read:

> "Remember our history, friends, and be warned. All our ancestors were led by the providential Cloud and taken miraculously through the Sea. They went through the waters, in a baptism like ours, as Moses led them from enslaving death to salvation life. They all ate and drank identical food and drink, meals provided daily by God. They drank from the Rock, God's fountain for them that stayed with them wherever they were. And the Rock was Christ. But just experiencing God's wonder and grace didn't seem to mean much—most of them were defeated by temptation during the hard times in the desert, and God was not pleased.
>
> "The same thing could happen to us. We must be on guard so that we never get caught up in wanting our own way as they did. And we must not turn our religion into a circus as they did—'First the people partied, then they threw a dance.' We must not be sexually promiscuous—they paid for that, remember, with 23,000 deaths in one day! We must never try to get Christ to serve us instead of us serving him; they tried it, and God launched an epidemic of poisonous snakes. We must be careful not to stir up discontent; discontent destroyed them.
>
> "These are all warning markers—DANGER!—in our history books, written down so that we don't repeat their mistakes. Our positions in the story are parallel—they at the beginning, we at the end—and we are just as capable of messing it up as they were. Don't be so naive

and self-confident. You're not exempt. You could fall flat on your face as easily as anyone else. Forget about self-confidence; it's useless. Cultivate God-confidence.

"No test or temptation that comes your way is beyond the course of what others have had to face. All you need to remember is that God will never let you down; he'll never let you be pushed past your limit; he'll always be there to help you come through it."

I just figured God could put things better than I could, and I thought it would be good for all of us to hear that.

I scanned the speech. I didn't take the time to absorb what the depth of the passage was about or to ponder the reasons why Jed had chosen it. I simply thought, *My son is getting a chance to speak to five thousand people, and all he wants to do is quote from God's Word. How cool is that?*

"We don't feel that this speech is really appropriate for a graduation ceremony," Principal Henson explained. "I'm sure in a church setting it would be fine, but this speech, as it is right now, just isn't…appropriate."

Without talking, my wife and I both looked toward Jed to gauge his sincerity and commitment in this. We deferred to Jed. We knew him, we trusted him, and this was his thing.

"Well, Jed," I asked, looking at him while shrugging my shoulders, "how important is this to you?"

Jed looked down at the desk and paused. I could see that tears were forming in his eyes and that he was squeezing his lips together. After a short silence, he looked up and stared at the principal.

With a quiet voice and with measured rhythm, he simply said, "That is the speech I want to give."

Wow, I thought in the moment. Apparently this matters quite a bit to him.

BACKSTORY

When Jed was six years old, he started playing ice hockey. Young hockey players spend a lot of time doing skating drills. Skating drills are not a whole lot of fun; they are by nature tedious and difficult. One of the early drills the kids do is to skate "C-cuts" up and down the ice, shifting each skate to its inner edge, propelling themselves in small semi-circles all the way to the goal line. Most kids would stick with their C-cuts about halfway down the ice and then gradually morph into a long-stride regular skating motion and race to the end. Not Jed. If the coach said to do C-cuts all the way to the end of the ice, that was what he did, even if it meant he finished last every time.

When Jed was in seventh grade his football coaches closed practice by telling the players to take a lap around the football field. I was one of those coaches. Sometimes I ran with them; sometimes I watched. Jed was one of few kids on the team who would literally not "cut corners." A football field is much smaller when you shave off the corners and run through the end zones. But if the coach said to run around the field, that was what Jed did. He would often finish last because he ran about forty yards farther than most of the other kids.

In the classroom it was the same way. Jed didn't waste his energy arguing or disputing with authority figures. It's a rare quality in a teenager and one he certainly did not genetically inherit from me. He finished high school having played on twelve sports teams, four different ones at the varsity level, and earning seven varsity letters. Jed was, in a word, *coachable*. And now, here he was before the authority figure of authority figures—the high school principal—and he was saying "no." Amazing.

DECISION

Mr. Henson let out a deep sigh. He hadn't asked for this dilemma, and he was clearly uncomfortable being put in the middle of it. He tried valiantly to convince Jed to change his mind. He explained how the valedictorian's assignment was to give a speech that talked about "life lessons." He explained how Jed's speech would be perfectly fine in a church setting, but might make people uncomfortable in a public graduation ceremony. He asked if Jed could just say something more like what the other students were saying.

My wife and I listened politely, but in our minds this was Jed's decision all the way. He had our support, whatever he decided.

Finally, after about fifteen minutes of Mr. Henson's suggestions, Jed looked up and quietly said, "Mr. Henson, if you force me to change my speech, then I guess I'll have to give a speech about why I wasn't allowed to say what I wanted to say."

That was pretty much the end of the meeting right there.

Mr. Henson let out another sigh. He seemed to know that this could be awkward for the school. I felt a bit sorry for him.

"I'll bring this to the superintendent and the school board, but I'm afraid that if you are not willing to reconsider you may not be allowed to speak at all," Mr. Henson warned.

The four of us left the meeting and went home. I told Jed that I thought it was fair for him to pray about this and consider what the school was asking of him, but that regardless of what he chose to do, his mom and I supported him fully. He told me that he was pretty sure he wasn't going to change his mind.

> **IT WAS BECOMING APPARENT TO ME THAT THE MESSAGE OF MY LIFE WAS, IN FACT, MAKING A DIFFERENCE IN THE LIFE OF MY SON.**

I thought I knew my son pretty well at that point in his life. We were close. We shared a lot of interests, and we spent a good amount of time together. It was becoming apparent to me that the message of my life was, in fact, making a difference in the life of my son.

I wanted my life to declare, reflect, and honor Christ. I wanted my family and my community to recognize that I was striving to live as a Christian. But that life message could not be imposed upon my kids; it can't be imposed upon anyone. Here, for maybe the first time, my son was now standing up and saying, "I am not ashamed of the Gospel of Jesus Christ." Wow.

For many years, I have been part of a Christian rock band known as Grooters & Beal. Dwight Beal and I recorded an album called *No Shame*. The title song was based on Romans 1:16. The chorus went:

> No shame, no I am not ashamed.
>
> No shame, of the Gospel or His name.
>
> It's the power of God, by which we all are saved,
>
> We need not be afraid…no shame.

Jed, in standing up for what he believed, even before a crowd of people at a high school graduation who may or may not have been open to his declaration of truth, was making a bold statement to all his friends and to his community. He was saying, without apology, "This is where I stand, and here is where I turn for truth." I was proud of him. I was pretty sure Jesus was, too.

DIDN'T SEE IT COMING

I thought I was paying attention to my family. I thought I was in step with my son, but I had not seen this coming.

Sitting in the principal's office that day, watching the humble determination of my own son, I was mildly shocked. *Jed wants to stand up for Jesus in front of his whole school? Where did this come from?* Jed had apparently been changing. His walk with the Lord had grown. This speech he wanted to give was not just a whim; it was a bold display of obedience, a public declaration before his friends, and a harbinger of his life's calling. Maybe our years of parenting and coaching and modeling and praying were actually working. I was watching my own son become a man and a kingdom leader right before my eyes.

> **I WAS WATCHING MY OWN SON BECOME A MAN AND A KINGDOM LEADER RIGHT BEFORE MY EYES.**

The next day, Thursday, I had a business trip that took me out of town. I found myself in a high-rise hotel in downtown Chicago, sitting in a comfortable chair, looking down at the relentless energy of South Wacker Drive. Something was gnawing at me. Jed's situation was stuck in my mind, and I couldn't shake it. I called him.

"What are you thinking?" I asked him.

"I'm fine," Jed said. "I don't think I should have to change my speech. I don't think I'm doing anything wrong."

"Okay," I answered him. "It is your decision, and I support you all the way. But do you mind if I tell a few people what is going on?"

Jed paused for a moment. "No, I think it is okay if you want to do that."

"Well, then I might just see if anyone else is interested in this story."

I hung up.

I typed up a short note outlining the essence of what was going on and emailed it to the news directors at two of our local Michigan newspapers: the *Grand Rapids Press* and the *Holland Sentinel*. Before I pressed the send button, I paused and said a short prayer.

"Lord, Your will be done."

Send.

I had no idea if I would hear anything back at all. It was late in the day, and I had never sent a "news tip" in my life. I thought, *Those guys probably don't even read their own email. This may go absolutely nowhere.* I thought that for about two minutes. Then the phone started ringing. They were more than interested. They wanted photos, details, and contact phone numbers. I gave it all to them.

The story exploded. It was front-page headline news. The AP picked it up. Jed was interviewed and photographed. The story went viral.

Valedictorian Asked Not to Give Speech that Quotes Interpretation of the Bible, read one headline.

West Ottawa Says Valedictorian Has to Change Speech, read another.

Soon we were getting calls from reporters, congressmen, lawyers, and even legal defense foundations. Jed was invited to read his speech on West Michigan's biggest radio news station. He went on the air and even took callers' questions and comments for nearly half an hour. Some supported him, some questioned him, but to each Jed calmly gave a rationale for his decisions. The host of the radio show explained that, while he himself didn't believe in the Bible, he defended Jed's right to quote from it if he chose.

We heard of a dozen pastors who took time the following Sunday morning to read Jed's speech—or should I say Paul's speech—verbatim to their congregations. Some called our home asking for a copy of his text.

"You already have it," we told them. "It's in First Corinthians chapter 10. Look it up."

But despite all the media attention, our local school superintendent, Patricia Koeze, would not budge. She was quoted in the newspaper saying, "We want to hear our valedictorians talk about their life lessons, but that's not what was coming from Jed. He was giving a religious speech."

Whether Jed was violating the Constitution of the United States became the subject of a fierce debate. Many people said that Jed's speech was inappropriate because of the "separation of church and state."

But in fact the words "separation of church and state" don't actually appear anywhere in the Constitution of the United States. What the First Amendment of the Constitution says is, "The Congress shall make no law respecting an *establishment* of religion, nor prohibiting the free exercise thereof." It is known as the "establishment clause." I could not fathom how allowing a eighteen-year-old valedictorian to say what he wanted to say in front of his own classmates for two minutes could possibly be construed as "Congress making a law respecting an establishment of religion." I mean, didn't we already have a law granting people the right to freedom of speech?

> **THE WORDS "SEPARATION OF CHURCH AND STATE" DON'T ACTUALLY APPEAR ANYWHERE IN THE CONSTITUTION OF THE UNITED STATES.**

Jed's classmates describe him as a humble guy, talented and good-natured. Jed's text for his valedictory address wasn't chosen in order to draw attention to himself or to his school. He certainly didn't anticipate the firestorm of media attention.

Newspapers as far from Michigan as Hawaii carried the story. Most of the articles I saw were well written, fact-based, and essentially neutral in their tone. The real fury came from the readers writing in the comments sections in the online versions of the papers. Jed's story generated hundreds and hundreds of spirited comments, and they were pouring in on each side of the issue.

In the Internet information age, communication is no longer one-way. Everyone has an opinion, and everyone has a voice. The majority of the feedback was affirming, encouraging, and wonderful, but some voices were critical, discouraging, and bitter.

THE HATE

> "...don't make these graduates suffer through a sermon most of them don't want to hear."

> "I believe that an (exiting) senior in high school should focus on the celebration at hand and not be so self important in the Valedictorian speech."

> "It's about time that West Michigan finally joined the rest of the civilized world and stopped cramming God down everyone's throat."

> "Religion doesn't have a place at a public school ceremony. There are plenty of ways to get the same message across."

> "Just because the majority of people in this area are self-proclaimed Christians doesn't mean that the U.S. Constitution can be ignored."

"Not everyone is Christian—get over it."

"He should have more than scripture to offer. If not, forget about it."

"LOL. I think someone needs to practice what they preach, i.e. arrogance."

"If you don't like it and want a country run by religion, move to Iran. See how you like it there!"

"In typical West Michigan fashion, the righteous always feel that they have to espouse their dogma as the most appropriate for everyone else. Courage? More like selfishness."

On Saturday, the day before graduation, our phone rang all day long. Many people wanted to talk to Jed—to thank him, to tell him he had inspired them, or to tell him they were pulling for him. Some of the people who called were folks he had never even met. Even our congressman, U.S. Representative Pete Hoekstra, called.

And where was Jed in the middle of this firestorm? He was playing basketball with his buddies, talking things over with his sister, and generally carrying on as if nothing much was happening.

A couple different legal defense attorneys who specialize in religious liberty issues told us that Jed's situation could warrant litigation. Previous American judicial decisions had ruled against students who wanted to pray or engage in what was termed proselytizing speech, but Jed's situation was different. Was simply quoting the Bible in school truly forbidden by the First Amendment? To ultimately decide this question, it may one day have to make it all the way to the Supreme Court. I was reminded of words I once heard from former Attorney General John Ashcroft, "Freedom of religion does not mean freedom *from* religion."

But Jed drew the line. He was not interested in lawsuits. He didn't want to hurt his school; he *loved* his school. He told the reporters, "I respect my school, and I love the people there. I'm not happy with their decision, but I will respect it."

GRADUATION DAY

On the morning of graduation, Jed met with the principal one last time. Once again, I did not know nor guide what he planned to do or say.

In the afternoon, my wife and I joined about five thousand people crammed into the bleachers of the gymnasium at West Ottawa High School. More than seven hundred graduates robed in black or white gowns sat in neat rows on the basketball court. The school band played, officials gave their introductory comments, and when it came time for the valedictorians to speak, one by one they took their place at the podium. There were five girls and four boys.

A young woman went first and gave a very nice and thoughtful reflection. Jed was up next. I wasn't sure if he was going to step to the microphone at all. The moment was electric and uncertain.

Jed stood up and approached the microphone. The crowd began to cheer. Someone yelled out, "Let him speak!" followed by more cheering.

Jed paused for a short moment for the ovation to die down. "You may have heard I will not be giving the speech I was going to give because it is inappropriate for a graduation setting," Jed said, eliciting some scattered boos. "I just want you to know that I love you and Jesus loves you, and that is the most important life lesson of all." That was it. Thunderous applause! A standing ovation! Jed had to wait a fair amount of time for the cheering to die down before he could introduce the next speaker.

> **"I JUST WANT YOU TO KNOW THAT I LOVE YOU AND JESUS LOVES YOU, AND THAT IS THE MOST IMPORTANT LIFE LESSON OF ALL.**

I was dumbfounded. I leaned over to Judy and said, "This is crazy. When I was a kid, the rebels always got the loudest cheers, but it never was rebels for Jesus!" I looked down at my son, who had humbly but firmly stood for his faith, for integrity, and for intellectual honesty. No shame.

The last of the valedictorians to speak that day was class president Andrew Webster. Webster was a successful athlete and a popular leader. Jed didn't know Andrew very well, they played different sports and mostly had different classes. Webster's original speech had been about the importance of focusing on the important things in life. We never heard that speech. As Andrew took his turn at the podium, he went off script. He said that, although he had prepared and submitted a speech, he had decided that he was going to instead use his time to let his classmates know who he really was and share a few of his favorite Bible verses.

He read:

I have told you these things so that in Me you may have peace. You will have suffering in this world. Be courageous! I have conquered the world (John 16:33 HCSB).

I know that all God does will last forever; there is no adding to it or taking from it. God works so that people will be in awe of Him (Ecclesiastes 3:14 HCSB).

Whoever loves money never has money enough; whoever loves wealth is never satisfied with his income. This too is meaningless (Ecclesiastes 5:10).

Naked a man comes from his mother's womb, and as he comes, so he departs. He takes nothing from his labor that he can carry in his hand (Ecclesiastes 5:15).

The instant Webster finished, the crowd burst into applause—but it was more than applause; it was cheering, exuberant cheering. I wondered what was behind this energy, this groundswell? These people couldn't all know Jed or Andrew personally. Was it coming from a frustration with a culture that was more and more openly hostile toward God? Was it an expression that they too were not ashamed of the Gospel? Whatever the motive, the vast majority of those in the gymnasium chose to affirm both Jed and Andrew.

Afterward it was reported by the local newspaper that school officials did not reprimand Andrew Webster for his speech. Principal Henson responded to inquiries from the press by saying, "What I'll say about that is one of our speeches went longer than what was planned, but overall the kids did a great job."

Andrew Webster later said in an interview for the press, "If they weren't going to let Jed speak, I figured I could."

Seven hundred kids at West Ottawa High School graduated that day. Jed was only one of them, but for him, the day was more than a graduation from high school; it was a coming of age. He had come face to face against the first obstacle that forced him to choose between obedience to his God and obedience to his culture. He made his choice clear, and in doing so he influenced, encouraged, and inspired thousands of others.

Following the ceremony, many of his classmates came up to him and threw their arms around him.

"Way to go."

"Way to stand up for what you believe in."

"I was proud of you today."

It didn't seem to matter if his friends were Christian, Buddhist, Muslim, Agnostic—one and all, they showed Jed their support. It seemed to me that the student body was far less afraid of the Bible than the school's lawyers, superintendent, and principal were.

In America, our culture is at a tipping point. Our Constitution is being reinterpreted to impose restrictions on the very thing it was originally meant to protect—the free exercise of religion and the freedom of speech. I'm not suggesting that we ought to live in a theocracy. I fully affirm that there should never be an official state religion. Look at history: that combination has never produced a society that was fair for all people. But Jed's speech shouldn't have been banned in a country that protects its freedoms the way the United States does. The same protections should be offered any citizen.

> **BY THE TIME MY SON WAS READY TO GRADUATE FROM HIGH SCHOOL HE WAS READY TAKE ON THE CHALLENGE BEFORE HIM WITH COURAGE AND FAITH.**

But the most interesting thing to me, as a father, was that by the time my son was ready to graduate from high school he was ready take on the challenge before him with courage and faith. That is, in my view, a modern frontier boy.

THE LOVE

I shared a few of the negative comments that came as a result of Jed's speech; now let me share a few of the positive ones.

> "Thanks be to God that these young men stood up for Christ! May those who were listening take to heart what they said because it is truth. May God bless you, Jed and Andrew, for your faithfulness to Him."

"Your actions will be used by God to touch many, including me! Thank you!"

"I was there, and these young adults should be able to say what they wanted. Neither boy was preaching to anyone, just stating what they got out of school and, more importantly, out of life so far. I had goose bumps hearing this in this setting. The school or whoever told Jed he had to change his speech is 100% wrong."

"Praising God for you Andrew and Jed! You are standing for truth and sharing what is the cornerstone of your lives. It reminds me of Joshua and Caleb. May God continue to bless you and guide you through college and beyond."

"I know Andrew and Jed took time to listen to the Spirit before writing and giving the speeches. Their words reflected God's true heart, and that is what matters. If some took offense to the words said, that is their right, yet I'm hoping the Spirit of God will touch them. There is only one true God. There is only one true Spirit. We need to reach out and understand other beliefs, yet we need to speak the word of Christ boldly! That is why I praise God for these 2 young men."

"If these were my boys I cannot tell you how immensely proud I would be of them! Actually I don't know them…and I'm still so proud. What an amazing display of character they showed! I hope they know they WILL be taken care of and blessed by God…more than they know!"

"It states in the Bible that 'if you are ashamed of me before men, then I will be ashamed of you before my Father.' And the way the guys stood up to pressure on this issue shows everyone that they ARE NOT

ASHAMED! Way to go! You are the talk of the neighborhood where I am...and in a good way!"

I was a proud father that graduation day, but not because of Jed's grade point average or his popularity among his classmates. I was proud that the message and calling of Jesus Christ had not been lost on my children. As my son took a public stand for Jesus, I became aware that, as parents, we are called to be multipliers of the kingdom, starting with our own kids.

> *The father of a righteous son will rejoice greatly, and one who fathers a wise son will delight in him* (Proverbs 23:24 HCSB).

JED'S SIDE OF THE STORY

I'd spent a lifetime hearing my dad talk about the Lord. The truth was around me and I wasn't opposed to it, but for whatever reason I wasn't ready to cling to it until my senior year of high school. I remember being seventeen and sitting in a Chinese restaurant with my dad and some missionary friends as they told stories about what God had been doing all over the world—powerful, miraculous things—and being affected by absolutely none of what was said.

But about six months later I realized that I had fallen pretty hard and needed to hear those stories again, this time letting them sink in. I don't know why it was the right time, but God simply opened my ears and I began to respond to the Spirit's call to search Him out. I got to the place where I had to confront it: If God is real—if God is who He says He is—then my life can't be what it is right now.

So I began reading Scripture on my own for the first time in my life and I began praying for the first time in my life—really. I became friends with people who knew the Lord. And appropriately, both suddenly and slowly, but very surely, the world became different. I became different.

Where was my dad in all this? Well, until graduation rolled around, he didn't really know the change that was happening in me. I had kept myself very hidden from him. He was as intentional and as good at keeping in contact with and knowing me as any dad that I've ever seen. But relationships always have to run two ways, and I had, for years, done a good job of hiding myself, largely because I didn't know myself. In any case, Dad didn't know about my relationship with God when it first began budding, and before that he didn't know about the sins I was wrapped up in.

> **I HAD SEEN A GOOD EXAMPLE OF WHAT SOMEONE WHO IS ZEALOUS FOR THE LORD LIVES LIKE. BECAUSE OF MY DAD'S LIFE, I WAS ENTERING TERRITORY THAT I RECOGNIZED.**

But he was involved, even though he didn't know it. Very involved. The significance of my dad's role in this whole ordeal is not necessarily one that can be spoken of in individual moments or chains of events, but is wrapped up in everything that had happened before that in my life—from birth until then. Even though I hadn't learned Scripture by my own study, even though I hadn't been a person of prayer by my own submission, and even though I had never been a person of much zeal or passion for anything in particular, when the Lord really did bring me to Him in a way that I hadn't known before, I realized that I had been prepared. I actually did know the Scripture. In a lot of ways, I did know how to pray. I had seen a good example of what someone who is zealous for the Lord lives like. Because of my dad's life, I was entering territory that I recognized.

The Lord was filling me with joy, with hope, and with a completely new perspective on life—defined by the revelation that He is actually God. And for the first time ever, I wanted people to *know* that He is actually God. My whole life, I would have been willing to politely debate with someone about why I was a Christian or why God existed or various things like that. But it was never important to me to tell people that God was God before. What had once been merely theoretical now had become quite real, and it mattered quite a bit. That is, that God is real.

THE SPEECH

I was new in all this, but I was excited. Graduation came around and I was getting a microphone. I really just wanted to say the Gospel, and I only had two minutes to share. I thought about telling my story or mentioning God in an episode of my life, but I couldn't figure out how to adequately express God's role and love in that amount of time. I didn't know what to do.

At some point, while my sister and I were talking and praying about it, we came to the conclusion that the Bible would be able to get to the point better than I would. There was probably a really good Scripture passage to read—I could read it and address it as need be.

We stumbled across Eugene Peterson's paraphrase of First Corinthians 10. Its message was exactly what I wanted to say: that God is actually the one God—the one who created us and bought us and redeemed us. I wanted my school to remember that we can't think too highly of ourselves. We can't go on sinning. And we can't think that God doesn't know us. He knows us, He's with us, and He's good. That was the reality I had just experienced in my life, and those were sincerely the words I wanted people to hear—just so that they didn't forget, so that they weren't unfamiliar with the Truth.

I was expecting no resistance. I figured my speech might not be similar to the speeches of the other valedictorians, but it didn't cross my mind that this would create conflict.

Sitting in the principal's office before I even had a chance to talk with my dad, I knew that I had his support and encouragement. I had become a confident person in general because of him and who he had been with me, and I had seen the message of his life: He proclaimed Jesus, and he focused on the truth and the creativity of our God and His Word. Whatever he thought about this speech, he was going to understand my heart.

I realize that this is a totally different circumstance than most kids have. Once this happened, like he said, he was just supportive—in more ways than I was paying attention to. And he was encouraging. He never took a stance that was not right behind me, and he never took a stance that was against anyone else, which really helped define where I was. I didn't want to stand aggressively anti-something or someone. I was definitely anti-sin, definitely anti-idolatry, but not anti-West Ottawa or anti-those who disagree with this passage of Scripture and my interpretation of it or anti-"the man." I was simply for the message of the Gospel, for my family and those who love me, and even for those who were against me. I was for life. My dad supported that stand, and like I said, it wasn't the specific moments that made the most impact; it was his consistency.

> **MY DAD SUPPORTED THAT STAND; IT WASN'T THE SPECIFIC MOMENTS THAT MADE THE MOST IMPACT—IT WAS HIS CONSISTENCY.**

There was a lot of discussion going around. I didn't feel really hurt or offended by the negative comments, but I was confused as to why people assumed certain things. And I was definitely upset when people who wanted me to speak responded negatively to those who said otherwise. A lot of people supported me purely for the sake of free speech, and I remember being sort of like, "Yeah, that's all right. But that's not at all what I care about here. Free speech is good, but Gospel speech is what I care about." Whether or not I could say what I wanted to say had nothing to do with what I was *saying*.

The First Corinthians passage is absolutely true. The Lord really carries you. This opposition I was facing for a graduation speech doesn't come close to the trials and tortures that many have faced. The Lord is faithful in all things, and I was pretty relaxed through the whole ordeal.

Being in front of people wasn't a problem—it wasn't really nerve-racking—but the standing ovation was kind of surreal. It was weird on the one hand for a lot of the same reasons that the free speech thing was weird, because some people were standing up for me largely because I "stuck it to the man." And again, that's not at all what I was after. Paul makes this very clear: The goal of preaching the Gospel is not that people cheer for you. What you want is an eruption for Christ, a standing ovation that comes from the realization that Jesus actually loves us. That should make us leap out of our seats and yell, "Yahoo!!"

But I also received support from a lot of truly genuine people—many people who stood up in the crowd were absolutely, sincerely grateful for what the Lord had done and that His Word was getting to be spoken. I was a product of the community they had developed by being faithful to the Lord—and that's worth a standing ovation, I think. So that was really cool. The mixture was the part that was surreal.

And then, of course, there was Andrew, who I totally respect and love.

Graduation turned me into someone who preached the Gospel. It was the first time that ever really happened, and it changed me for good. Once you stand up on stage and say, "This is my God" in a loud and clear voice, and not only "This is my God," but "This *is* God" and "This is Truth," you actually have to carry the message and continue to give it. As far as I'm concerned, if you stop carrying that message after you've declared it, it's worse for your sake than if you had never spoken it at all. Graduation gave me deeper confidence in the faithfulness of God. This whole episode of life became a testimony of His faithfulness.

> **AS FAR AS I'M CONCERNED, IF YOU STOP CARRYING THAT MESSAGE AFTER YOU'VE DECLARED IT, IT'S WORSE FOR YOUR SAKE THAN IF YOU HAD NEVER SPOKEN IT AT ALL.**

And, my relationship with my dad changed. I changed, and he was not left unchanged by the change in me because we're directly connected. And now we know each other better. Even though there was still some of me hidden after that, there was a whole lot of me uncovered. I learned new things about my dad and his faith because he realized that I was actually concerned about it, and he learned about me because my life was being brought into light. All of a sudden, we had newness, and we had new things to talk about.

PRACTICING PRINCIPLES

*Principle #1: Declare your allegiances publicly;
your kids are watching.*

How would you rate yourself in declaring your allegiances publicly and privately in front of your children? Do they see the best in you more often than the worst? What steps can you take today to improve that rating—to ensure that you are a living example of what you believe?

CHAPTER 2
BACKSTORY

Principle #2: Live a life worthy of your calling.

Lots of people I meet hate Michigan winters. Not me. I grew up in the desert of Scottsdale, Arizona, and I hated summer. In August the temperature would sometimes hit 120 degrees in the Valley of the Sun. That kind of heat is meant only for the devil and his angels. I guess that's why Arizona State is called the Sun Devils.

But my family, mercifully, took me out of the desert and brought me to the Promised Land. When I was fourteen years old, my dad told us that we were moving to a small town in Northern Michigan, a town called Charlevoix. He showed me on the map how Charlevoix was surrounded by lakes, was near the forty-fifth parallel, and had major ski hills within an hour's drive.

I was ready to go. For one thing, I'd spent my whole life trying to establish my reputation in the world, and I wasn't sure I had done a very good job of it. I welcomed the chance to start over. For another thing, gangs were forming in my high school, and I'd already been jumped twice. The place was getting increasingly dangerous. I couldn't leave soon enough.

It was the age of Boston's new hit song "More Than a Feeling," and for me, it was like a rebirth. My mother, on the other hand, was not quite as excited. Scottsdale, Arizona, was a great place for her. She taught at the local college, had a lot of great friends, and was sewn into the fabric of an up-and-coming community that was fast becoming a desirable shopping destination. Somehow, I didn't quite see the value of any of those perks.

It took our family four days to caravan across the country toward our new home. It was the Northern Migration—and definitely out of step with national trends in the early days of the Carter administration. My mom, dad, younger sister, and younger brother rode in our family's 1970 Volkswagen Campmobile—certifiably the slowest vehicle ever made. I rode shotgun with a young dude from Charlevoix named Bud Boss (I had never met anyone named "Bud" before) in our family's sweet 1973 Dodge Dart. The Dart had four cylinders of Detroit muscle, and we used them all pulling our fifteen-foot speedboat that was stuffed with all the junk that hadn't made it onto the moving truck. I'm surprised we even made it to New Mexico.

It was January when we made the trip. January is a gentle, tender month in Arizona. But in Northern Michigan January is an entirely different beast. It was dark and snowing when we finally arrived in Petoskey, Michigan, after the final thirteen hours on the road. Petoskey is actually twenty miles north of Charlevoix. Apparently they did not have hotels in Charlevoix—at least not cheap hotels. As I dragged my aching body off the vinyl seats of the Dart, I stepped into a world of frigid temperatures and sideways blowing snow. I had always presumed that snow fell gently downward, like it did in the snow globes. I didn't know that snow could fall sideways and feel like razor shards against your skin. My mother was crying.

> **THIS WAS GOING TO BE "MORE THAN A FEELING."**

But I was not crying. My aversion to the demonic heat of the Arizona summers led me to make a pledge to myself. I pledged that I would never, ever complain about the coldness of winter, but would instead try to find new ways to enjoy the season. Learning to snow ski was first on my list. This was going to be "More than a Feeling."

ON THE SLOPES

Our last Christmas in Arizona had been just a few weeks before we were scheduled to move. Under the tree that Christmas were two long presents with my name on them. My parents, who knew absolutely nothing about snow skiing, had bought me a used pair of wooden Tempest snow skis, a pair of used LOOK bindings, and a brand-new pair of lime-green Garmont ski boots. Although I had never been on a real ski hill, I assumed that standing on my skis in the living room and digging my ski poles deep into the brown shag carpet qualified as "lessons." In my mind I was in Innsbruck, Austria, racing Franz Klammer for Olympic Gold.

The first weekend after we had moved into our new home, I asked my dad to bring me out to the slopes. In Charlevoix the slopes consist of a very small municipally-run ski hill called Mt. McSauba. Served by two rope tows, Mt. McSauba cost five bucks for a lift ticket and thirty bucks for the suede glove liners that were essential if you didn't want the rope to tear up your gloves.

On my maiden voyage to Mt. McSauba I wasn't planning to risk the rope tow. My dad agreed to push me partway up the hill and let me slide down a little ways, just to get the feel of things. So my dad put two hands in the small of my back and pushed me about thirty yards up the gentlest slope you can imagine. If you had dropped a soccer ball where we stopped, the ball would have paused to think for a moment before it decided to roll down the hill.

But I had never really stood on skis before. I was an Arizona kid. I didn't know how to turn, how to stop, or how to use a rope tow, so this arrangement seemed pretty good to me. For about an hour my dad—God bless him—patiently walked up and down the hill while I went "skiing."

To my left and to my right other skiers were flying around, hitting jumps, whipping snow as high as a wall as they spun their Olin, Hexcel, or K2 skis and came to abrupt stops. I didn't notice anyone else skiing on wooden Tempests that day. I wondered if I would ever learn to make a cool stop like that. And while I was watching all these alpine masters, it never once occurred to me that these were the same kids who were about to become my classmates. It also never occurred to me how ridiculous I looked.

I was undeterred. I soon became an eager student for any pretty young girl who was willing to give me skiing instruction. It was a pretty effective method of meeting new girls. "Hey—you really seem like you know how to ski. What's your name?" Eventually I mastered the art of the rope tow.

I still love to ski. For many years after college I took annual ski trips with two of my best friends, Dwight Beal and Kevin Harney. We always went where they had real mountains, real snow, and serious vertical, and for us that meant west. When we first started taking these annual treks Kevin was a young pastor and Dwight and I were actively traveling with our band, Grooters & Beal. We bought lift tickets at great places like Breckenridge, Heavenly, Sun Valley, Kirkwood, Alta, Copper Mountain, Keystone, Sierra, and Squaw Valley. We traveled cheap, booked the lowest cost motels we could find, fed ourselves at all-you-can-eat salad bars, and tried to discover a new mountain every year.

We were actually interested in more than just skiing. Every one of our western trips also became a spiritual retreat and God-seeking time. We took seriously the business of sharing our lives and seeking God's will for our future. We spent time in prayer.

Sometimes we wrote Bible verses on index cards and memorized them on the chairlifts. We usually brought a guitar and strummed out a few worship songs at night. The fellowship made the skiing even better. I began to associate skiing with growing closer to God, deepening friendships, and being intentional about my life.

> **SOMETIMES WE WROTE BIBLE VERSES ON INDEX CARDS AND MEMORIZED THEM ON THE CHAIRLIFTS.**

After five years of the Rockies and the Sierra Nevada mountains we set a goal to ski the Swiss Alps. Grooters & Beal was doing a lot of music in those days, and our booking agent, Kim, spent a month every summer working at the United Nations in Geneva, Switzerland. Dwight and I challenged Kim to find us a booking somewhere in Switzerland that winter. We generously offered to play anywhere, anytime, in exchange for a week's lodging near an Alp. To our amazement, Kim came through.

We were introduced to the Crossroads Church in Ferney, France, an English-speaking congregation that is connected to an organization called Crossroads International. The Crossroads Church, in association with the local chapter of Youth for Christ, agreed to put us to work. They organized a concert in the city of Lyon, invited us to lead worship on Sunday morning, arranged for us to play on Friday night in a local coffee bar in Geneva, and even got us into some local schools to play and talk about music. In order to seamlessly blend with the culture, we got hold of some French language instructional cassette tapes and learned to say key phrases in French like, *"Je ne comprends pas."* Translation: "I do not understand what you are saying because you are speaking in French, and I don't understand French because I am an American, and therefore, I only speak English." It's a very helpful phrase.

In exchange for our music, the church took care of our lodging and made us feel welcome. At the end of our ministry weekend we hitched a ride to a ski condo in a little alpine village called Combloux. I just love saying that word: *Combloux*. I really love saying any French word.

In Combloux we soon learned the shuttle and bus schedules and were able to hitch rides to some of the most beautiful places I had ever seen—the French Alps near Mt. Blanc. We skied at places with cool French names like Les Contamines Montjoie, Chamonix, and Les Houches. Go ahead and say them out loud in your best Inspector Clouseau voice. It's fun. We ate lots of melted cheese and developed a raging appetite for fondue and raclette. At night we strolled through quaint and charming villages like Megev amidst twinkling lights, ancient churches, art galleries, outdoor skating rinks, gourmet chocolatiers, and wooden outdoor crepes booths. Dwight and Kevin were decent company, but this place had serious romantic potential!

The combination of ministry and skiing was hard to beat. We were hooked.

> **BUT ON EVERY TRIP WE REMAINED INTENTIONAL ABOUT TAKING INVENTORY OF OUR LIVES, LISTENING TO THE VOICE OF GOD, AND SEEKING HIS WILL FOR OUR FUTURES.**

Over the years we made five trips back to visit our friends in the Ferney Church, always combining skiing and ministry. The nature of the ministry changed over the years as Kevin became a well-known speaker and author. In the early years Grooters & Beal did music and Kevin more or less just tagged along, but by the fourth and fifth year Kevin was being invited to do speaking and teaching and Dwight and I were along mostly to carry his extra books in our suitcases. But on every trip we remained intentional about taking inventory of our lives, listening to the voice of God, and seeking His will for our futures.

With that as my background, it is no wonder that my wife and I stopped having kids after two. Back then most chairlifts were designed to carry only four people. Four seemed to me to be the perfect number for a family. Should we have another? No. We couldn't very well leave one kid off the chairlift, could we? In retrospect, I'm not sure that was the most solid reasoning. But I did know that one day I wanted to transfer my love of skiing to my own family.

As soon as our own kids could walk we hauled them to the mountains. They weren't going to be embarrassed the way I was by making it to the teenage years without learning so much as a snowplow. Gradually the annual ski trips with my buddies were replaced by annual ski trips with my own family, and it wasn't long till both our kids could ski circles around me.

> **YOU GATHER AT THE TOP OF THE MOUNTAIN, SAY HELLO AND HAVE AN OPENING PRAYER.**

I wanted to share with my family the association I had experienced between skiing and spiritual growth. We discovered that some mountains have "skiing pastors" who hold Sunday worship services right on the slopes. It's not a bad way to do it. You gather at the top of the mountain, say hello and have an opening prayer. Then off you go and you ski down to some beautiful spot and sing a song or something. Then down you go to some quiet little alcove where the mountain pastor reflects a little on a Bible passage. I figure the most beautiful sanctuary we ever went to church in was on the back slopes of Snowmass on a blue sky Sunday morning.

THE START OF A STORY

By the time Jed was twelve years old, a friend of mine offered me a few days in his timeshare condo in Whistler, Canada. We planned a ski trip for just Jed and me—a five-day father-son Canadian adventure. Little did we know that that trip was going to be a catalyst for what would ultimately become *The Frontier Boys*.

The great thing about skiing is that on chairlifts you are practically forced to talk to one another. No matter how fast the lifts run you are inevitably going to spend a lot more time riding up than you are skiing down. And chairlifts are quiet. If you don't bring cell phones or earbuds, the chairlift can be a place where you can experience the peaceful serenity of winter. The lift silently carries you above snow-covered trees, rocky outcrops, and wide open alpine valleys. The chairlift is one of the most spectacular and scenic rides you could ever find—and it's all out in the fresh air. So if you're looking for quality time with your twelve-year-old, this is it.

On the Whistler trip I suggested to Jed that we spend some of our time concocting a story. Jed was an avid reader and I wanted to see where we might go if we pretended we were going to write a book together. Would our story be science fiction or fantasy? Fiction or non-fiction? What would keep his interest? Who would be his hero? So we began coming up with crazy "what if" statements.

"What if there were space aliens who came to earth and abducted all the dogs and cats of the world?"

"What if there was a massive typhoon that grew out of Lake Michigan and wiped out Wisconsin?"

"What if you had the power to secretly make people fart whenever you wanted them to? Wouldn't that be cool? You could totally embarrass anybody!"

In a brainstorm, anything is fair game.

Ultimately we settled onto a story about four characters who were best friends, who were about Jed's age, who were great athletes, and who got into a big mess. We talked about what might happen if one of them got mixed up with the wrong crowd. We talked about what it would be like to have your best friend die, but still send you instant messages. We talked about what it might be like to be the only person who knew your best friend was not really dead.

And on and on we went. There was no end game in mind; this was not an assignment—it was just passing the time on the chairlift. We kept at it for a couple of days, then we moved on.

By the way, that was the same ski trip where we conceived of designing a video game where people who didn't really know how to play the guitar could play simulated guitars alongside real rock and roll songs. Imagine our surprise when *Guitar Hero* came out two years later!

The following winter I went back to Switzerland, this time just with Kevin Harney, and we spent a lot of time on that trip writing. I took the nugget of the story that Jed and I had discussed and began to write it down. Kevin was working on what would become the first of his published books, a non-fiction book called *Finding a Church You Can Love and Loving the Church You Found*.

My story was all fiction, but *The Frontier Boys* were coming to life. As Kevin and I read our pages out loud to one another we swapped ideas, critiques, and encouragements. I kept thinking about the primary audience I was trying to reach—twelve-year-old Jed. As I was writing I kept asking myself, *What was I willing to read when I was twelve years old?* And, *How can I season an adventure story with something true and inspiring from the Bible without making it feel forced in?*

I had been studying the messages our kids were receiving through the popular books, music, television, and film of our culture. I was concerned about the impact that years and years of those messages were having on Jed's generation. I didn't like what I found, but I found no hope in just becoming a critic. I had to try and create something else, something different, something true. I wanted to speak loudly with a compelling voice of counterculture, like a guitar amplifier of truth, blasting in a way that made you tap your foot and pay attention. As Paul says in Ephesians 4:1, "…I urge you to live a life worthy of the calling you have received." The question was, could I?

I found out that American boys were slipping in nearly every category. Trends that have blossomed in the second decade of this millennium were being incubated in the first. Boy's scores in school were dropping across the board. The percentage of boys in college was already way below the percentage of girls, and it was dropping. Boys' participation in team sports was falling, but video game sales were going through the roof. The percentage of thirty-year-old men living with their parents was higher than it had been in one hundred years. Something big was happening in our culture —we were losing the men. When my father was a kid in the 1940s and 1950s he read Hardy Boys and Sugar Creek Gang books. He watched Roy Rogers on television. His boyhood heroes had an intrinsic sense of valor and courage, and there was distinct clarity between right and wrong. By the 2000s any sort of moral clarity was now suspect. Truth was relative. God was most closely associated with self-actualization. Tolerance was king, regardless of what you were tolerating.

> **HIS BOYHOOD HEROES HAD AN INTRINSIC SENSE OF VALOR AND COURAGE, AND THERE WAS DISTINCT CLARITY BETWEEN RIGHT AND WRONG.**

And I looked for role models—heroes who defeat evil through great courage or valor, who overcome incredible obstacles, and who inspire boys to become better than they thought they could be. All I found was Grand Theft Auto, Eminem, and MTV.

The early adolescent years are, for most guys anyway, the most confusing, threatening, and challenging years of life. At that age we are all inherently insecure. You look at yourself in the mirror and you see yourself as either too skinny or too fat. And at school, which you are, of course, forced to go to, the law of the jungle prevails. In the law of the jungle the strong prey on the weak, and there will inevitably be stronger predators than you. You can't escape the law of the jungle in the seventh grade based on brains or cunning. Nobody escapes. Everybody is forced into the same structured Darwinian social network.

But junior high is also the time when boys begin to recognize that they have the freedom to chart their own course through life. Regardless of what the grown-ups think, junior high kids know how to do all the vices. They know how to drink, how to smoke, how to take drugs, and how to have sex. The stupidest term in the world is *Adult Entertainment,* as if you have to be an adult to be entertained by sexual content. It should be called *Adolescent Entertainment* because it's never more entertaining than when your hormones are just starting to explode.

But junior high is also a time where a boy's soul is uncommitted and open to the Holy Spirit. Junior high ministries understand the need for high-energy activities and near-constant stimulation, but the good ones also know that there is plenty of space in kids' hearts for the life-changing presence of God. I certainly didn't understand the full depth of what I was doing when, as a twelve-year-old, I laid in my bunk bed at Huachuca Oaks camp in Southeastern Arizona and prayed, "God, if I've never really opened my heart to You, I want to do that tonight."

> "GOD, IF I'VE NEVER REALLY OPENED MY HEART TO YOU, I WANT TO DO THAT TONIGHT."

It was pretty dry as far as conversion stories go, but it was a critical starting point for the intention of my heart. It was God-initiated, certainly, and subsequently fed by many waters, but in that bunk bed at that little camp I made sure to claim Jesus for myself. I'll never forget it. I remember knowing that God was listening, even if no one else was.

Decisions made in early adolescence change the shape of lives, and as awesome as many church and para-church ministries are at reaching out to junior high kids, they are hopelessly outgunned by the armies of our culture. Even the best ministries get their kids' attention for only an hour a week, maybe two. The culture gets unfettered access for every other waking moment.

One of my favorite quotes is attributed to Michelangelo, who once said, "Don't criticize, create," or as I've also seen it quoted, "criticize by creating." So rather than just criticizing the messages or messengers of a secular culture, I believed the greater challenge was to create competing messages. Join the fray and point to God with art and music, and welcome the competition for attention. I had been trying to *be* that competing message for Jed—now we together would try to put the guitar amplifier to a new story, to make it louder and bigger.

> **JOIN THE FRAY AND POINT TO GOD WITH ART AND MUSIC, AND WELCOME THE COMPETITION FOR ATTENTION.**

It took eight years for the story of *The Frontier Boys* to move from chairlift to silver screen, but like any tall tree, it had to start as a seed and it had to grow. I was interested in nurturing that particular seed because I thought *The Frontier Boys* had the potential to introduce modern heroes with authentic faith in Jesus. To bring characters like that to life within a culture where young media role models were practically invisible—now that felt like a calling.

JED'S SIDE OF THE STORY

Getting off of the ski hill and peeling off your ski boots and snow pants is one of the most wonderful experiences ever. Of course, waking up and being able to put all that stuff on and go on a hill is also great. Then you ski all day, you're freezing, the stuff is heavy on your body, you're really tired, and you come back to this warm place knowing that very shortly you will take all the weight off, get cozy, be with family, and eat the most magnificent dinner you can imagine. Ultimate vacation.

I always understood spring break as a winter trip. Our family never, ever went to beaches or anything for spring break—we always went someplace cold—so I thought that's what everyone did. And I loved it. I was rollerblading by the time I was three and playing ice hockey by six, so skiing on snowblades was natural for me. If you haven't seen snowblades before, they are like very short skis that you buckle on and go. No poles necessary. They are like ice skates for the slopes. As a twelve-year-old, my goal was to find the highest, hardest slope and go straight for that one, which is the stage I was in on this particular trip with Dad.

I didn't talk much during middle school; I was not perfectly secure with myself. I didn't really know what I was doing with life besides trying to do well in school, make sports teams, and have some fun. Skiing with Dad was fun, especially compared to the social setting that I spent most of my time in.

I never played water polo, but I have friends who did. In water polo, if you can get away with grabbing someone's ankle and pulling him backward to thrust yourself forward, you do it. It's the most frustrating thing in the world when your ankle gets grabbed, or your shoulder, and you get pulled back. And that was kind of what middle school was like—everyone just grasping to pull others back and pull themselves up. Crazy effort and frustrating pullbacks.

> **DAD WAS ONE OF VERY FEW PLACES I COULD GO AND FEEL SOCIALLY COMFORTABLE AND SAFE, BE EXCITED AND ENCOURAGED, AND FEEL GOOD ABOUT WHO I WAS.**

So my relationships with family were refuge relationships. Dad was one of very few places I could go and feel socially comfortable and safe, be excited and encouraged, and feel good about who I was. Dad is not what I would consider the "strong, silent" type. He's constantly in conversation, constantly thinking up ideas for games or stories or whatever else is creatable.

Growing up, Dad would make up stories for my sister and me constantly. When we were very young, he told us a story every night before bed. It was always a new story; it always had some semblance of my sister and me in it; and it always ended well. So it wasn't unusual that we would be making up stories on the chairlifts. Since I wasn't very interested in talking about my own world, making up a world of other characters was a good way to engage. And I remember being entertained enough by the process that we continued the story-making as I peeled off my snow pants and plopped down inside the hotel room.

PRACTICING PRINCIPLES

Principle #2: Live a life worthy of your calling.

How convinced are you of your calling as a parent? What exactly does your calling mean to you? Can you sincerely identify yourself as "called" to be a parent? Does your life reflect your calling?

CHAPTER 3
COMPETITIVE EDGE

*Principle #3: Enter your son's world,
and include him in yours.*

I realize that not everyone likes or is cut out for sports, but I have always loved them. I have to be careful not to let my passion for sports become an idol in my life. I often justify my interest and obsession with games, statistics, fantasy leagues, and the like by saying that it's cheaper than counseling. I am able to distance my brain from the stresses of business and the anxieties of life by dropping temporarily into the world of sports. By relaxing my brain into the familiar and trivial world of games and standings, I am able to later re-engage with the things that matter with renewed energy. At least, that's what I tell my wife.

I am not alone in this passion for distraction. I remember the day the Entertainment and Sports Network (ESPN) came on the air (or the cable, if we want to be accurate) for the first time. I was in college, and I was doing some sports broadcasting for my school, Hope College. I briefly considered dropping out of school, jumping in my car, and driving from Holland, Michigan, to Bristol, Connecticut, to try to catch on with this new network. ESPN sounded like everything I wanted to do with my life. At the time they had almost nothing to show on the network. I think they were broadcasting curling. I figured ESPN would never catch on, so I stayed in school.

When I was a kid in Scottsdale, Arizona, I loved to play basketball in the driveway, baseball on the Little League fields, football at the Boys Club, street hockey with my buddies, tennis at the community college, and golf on the local municipal course. I was the first kid on my block with urethane skateboard wheels, and I still have a vintage copy of the first edition of *Skateboarder Magazine*. I ran track for my school, went surfing at Big Surf (a local waterpark), took my Hart slalom water ski out to the lake any chance I got, read dozens of sports biographies, collected baseball cards by the shoebox-full, and never, ever missed Monday night football. I was in my mid-forties when I met Frank Gifford at a charity auction event. He autographed a football for me. I told him that I had seen more of his television broadcasts than any living person. He thought I was just being nice.

I credit (or blame) my love of sports to two men. First, I credit my dad. Though not a fanatic, he was a good athlete—basketball in particular—and he was always willing to shoot hoops or play catch with me. Second, I had a fantastic P.E. coach all through elementary school. Coach Pete Howell of Mohave Elementary School in Scottsdale, Arizona was the Vince Lombardi of my young life. Tough, fair, and tireless, Coach Howell coached the track team, the basketball team, the flag football team, and all the P.E. classes. He was a man who made athletic competition fair and fun. He taught us everything from badminton to bowling, from the Fosbury flop to fly fishing. I think I remember every compliment he ever paid me because you really had to earn a compliment from Coach Howell. He was a great influence on my life, although I didn't fully appreciate his excellence as a teacher at the time.

> **THESE TWO MEN STAMPED ME WITH A LOVE AND APPRECIATION FOR ATHLETICS, TEAM SPORTS, AND COMPETITIVE GAMES.**

These two men stamped me with a love and appreciation for athletics, team sports, and competitive games. It was a stamp that I was inevitably going to try and place on my son, should I ever have one. On March 27, 1990, we had one. Jedidiah John Grooters was born in the Holland Hospital, ten minutes from our little house. Driving to the hospital on the day he was born I started singing a song to myself. I couldn't help it.

I got a little boy, and his name is Jedidiah.

I'll teach him how to throw and how to sing in the choir.

And he will grow up big and strong.

And I will be there all along.

And that is why I sing this song.

Because Jed and I are gonna hang around, I say,

Thank You, Lord, thank You, Lord,

Thank You, Lord, for my little boy,

Thank You, Lord, well thank You, Lord—

I thank You for my little boy.

I used to sing it to him every night before he went to sleep. I realize from the lyrics of that little song that it never occurred to me that my son might not actually like sports or want to learn how to throw a ball. "The Jedidiah Song" was actually the second-to-last song of the night. The very last song came from the Beverly Hillbillies.

Well, let me tell a story 'bout a man named Jed....

Writing songs about my kids was natural, and I had written a real syrupy one for our daughter Jordyn when she was born. We recorded that song on a Grooters & Beal album called *Simple Life*. For Christmas one year my kids had the lyrics of these corny songs printed on baseball shirts. Hilarious. Sometimes really corny things are actually the most touching. Don't tell them I said that.

GETTING INTO THE GAME OF GOLF

My own parents never pushed me into sports, and I didn't want to become one of those overbearing sports dads either. I've seen plenty of fathers who try to live vicariously through their sons, who are driven to make it to the top of the athletic heap through their kids in ways they may have never been able to achieve on their own. I didn't want to be that guy.

> **THERE IS A TRUE SATISFACTION THAT COMES FROM COMPETENCY. LEARNING A NEW SKILL AND EXCELLING AT IT IS INHERENTLY SATISFYING.**

But at the same time, I sometimes wished my dad had pushed me a little harder, challenged me a little more. After all, there is a true satisfaction that comes from competency. Learning a new skill and excelling at it is inherently satisfying. Of course the other possibility is that too much pushing from the parents often kills any enjoyment their kids might have derived from sports.

I thought about this when my kids were still very small. Would I push them? Would I sit back and let them discover their own interests organically? I decided to expose my children to sports, play with them, give them opportunities, and teach them skills as best I could. If they showed interest and aptitude, we would take the next step; if not—well, then that would be fine, too.

Take golf, for example. I love golf and am always eager for a new excuse to get out and play. Taking my young son golfing was foolproof. He was only about four years old when we first started golfing together. We incorporated a method of mild competition that made every round focused, but not too stressful. My friend, Kevin, suggested it to me one day.

"Drop your son off at the red marker 100 yards from the green and let him hit from there. Give him two free strokes a hole, and play him for skins."

So I did. Skins are simply a way of scoring where rather than tallying total strokes over nine or eighteen holes, you treat each hole as win, lose, or draw and keep track of how many holes, or skins, you win versus your opponent. At age five, Jed could easily smack a golf ball along the ground from 100 yards and get it to the green in two or three strokes, and he could putt pretty well, too. Our skins games were pretty close—and there was always something at stake. At the end of the round, whoever had won the most skins got to choose the beverage that the other had to drink. When he beat me, I usually ended up drinking something blue or pink.

As Jed got older and better, he moved back to the white 150-yard markers, then to the blue 200-yard markers, then to the ladies tees. All those years, he retained his two strokes-a-hole handicap. Eventually, he moved back to the men's tees, then he lost a stroke, then he lost his other stroke. By the time he became a top golfer on his high school team I started asking him if I could hit from the ladies tees or the 150-yard marker.

Golf is the best game I know of to reveal character. I learn more about a guy on the golf course than anywhere else. Is he essentially an optimist or a pessimist? You will find out on the golf course. Is he self-centered or other-centered? You will find out on the course. How does he handle adversity? Adversity is inevitable in golf. Is he honest? None of these attributes have much to do with how good a player he is or with how low a score a person can post.

For me, golf is like skiing; it is a chance to be in nature. Golf courses are beautiful places. I know that the Psalmist wasn't envisioning a fairway when he wrote the 23rd Psalm: "He makes me lie down in green pastures, he leads me beside quiet waters" (Ps. 23:2). I've spent time in the Judah wilderness, and I have seen the geographical context of those words. The green pastures the Psalmist writes about are nothing more than a few sporadic tufts of grass that emerge in the morning along the western edge of small rocks on a desert hillside. But for me "green pastures" brings to mind an early morning, dew on the grass, fog dissipating off the surface of the pond, round of golf. For me golf is beautiful, challenging, and character-building. Of course I wanted to share it with my son.

From early on, I could tell that Jed's character was well-suited for golf. In all the years I've played golf with Jed, I've never heard him raise his voice or get mad. He's never thrown a club. At the high school level he played some pretty competitive golf. He won some, he lost some—but he played the game because it was enjoyable. He embodies the phrase *playing golf.* It is supposed to be play. Even though tough competition can make the play more focused, it is still play.

> **EVEN THOUGH TOUGH COMPETITION CAN MAKE THE PLAY MORE FOCUSED, IT IS STILL PLAY.**

This is the role that sports played for me in the raising of a son. Sports were an excuse, a reason, a space, and an opportunity for us to hang out together, to get to know each other, and to work together toward a common pursuit.

Sports became an acute interest of Jed's, but that interest had to be planted. It was up to us to buy him his first Rollerblades®, and he enjoyed skating on those things as soon as he was old enough to stand up. His first word was *ball*. He was walking at nine months; at one, he was swinging at WIFFLE® balls in the front yard.

But playing games in the front yard and joining an adult-led organized team sport are two very different things. Jed was five years old when I suggested he might like to play on a T-ball team. To my surprise, he didn't really want to do it. It was easier to stay home where everything was comfortable than to get dragged out to a field with a bunch of kids he didn't know to try his hand at something new like T-ball.

Every kid and every situation is different, but for Jed at age five I really thought he would enjoy and benefit from the experience of a team. How could he know if he would enjoy it? He had no frame of reference for such an experience. On a real team a young guy can learn valuable lessons, especially if he has a good coach. A team can teach a boy that everything isn't always only about him. On a team he must learn to take turns; everyone doesn't get to bat at the same time.

After one season of T-ball I realized I needed to do more than just attend the games—I needed to help out. For the next eight years I volunteered, like so many dads do, to coach Little League baseball. I also signed up to coach football and became an assistant coach for many years in the youth hockey program.

Most of my non-working life became structured around the schedule of practices and games. My wife coached our daughter, as they both got involved with AAU Volleyball. Like many families, we spent nearly every weekend and many evenings hanging out at hockey rinks, high school gymnasiums, or baseball fields.

> **IT IS TRICKY TO FIND THE RIGHT BALANCE WITH KIDS' ACTIVITIES—THERE HAVE TO BE LIMITS.**

It is tricky to find the right balance with kids' activities—there have to be limits. Kids shouldn't be involved in every possible thing and have commitments every single night of the week; but organized activities can serve as a helpful boundary line for your own calendar. Sports schedules helped me to say no to a thousand things that really were optional in my own life. I often found it tempting to stay at work and put in extra time, but the formal structure of the practice or the game gave me the impetus I really needed to put family time in a place of priority. I was employed until my son turned eleven, and then I opened a small business. In each case, I enjoyed my work and gladly worked long hours. But I thank God that my kids' sports teams came along and helped me carve out time when I would be with them doing "their" things. Baseball practice, hockey games, golf leagues, and volleyball and tennis matches had the pull to supersede almost anything on my to-do list. Sports opened a connection point where I could enter my son's world, and I'm glad for that.

GET INVOLVED TOGETHER

There are hundreds of other potential connection points as well. We tried music, for example. Jed signed up for drum lessons with a fantastic drum teacher. He did exceptionally well at his lessons, but he never developed a passion to play the drums. He eventually tired of the school band as well. For me as a kid music was a big deal. I was in garage bands starting in about fifth grade. But for my son it was not a huge interest. That was fine; we gave him a taste. It may be Scouts; it may be science fairs; it may be sailing or fishing. I hope it's not video games—but whatever it is, it's imperative for fathers to enter their sons' worlds. Get close. Learn the terminology. Have something you can talk about together.

Jed made this easy on me because he loved to play sports. He did not, however, obsess over them. He had talent, hand-eye coordination, and cool disposition under pressure. He didn't get despondent after losses or cocky after wins. These are great qualities in sports, and, really, in life!

> **HE DIDN'T GET DESPONDENT AFTER LOSSES OR COCKY AFTER WINS. THESE ARE GREAT QUALITIES IN SPORTS, AND, REALLY, IN LIFE!**

One year we were cruising through our Little League baseball summer with a really good team. I had a great group of parents, a team of kids I knew well, and a lineup that was balanced from top to bottom. We had two pitchers who couldn't be beat, Jed and Greg. Little League has strict rules about how many innings a young arm can pitch and how many days of rest they need between pitching outings. I followed those rules to the letter, but I pitched Jed and Greg as much as they were allowed to pitch. At one point in the season Jed was 10-0 and Greg was 9-1. Then Jed's arm got sore. We shut him down and lost in the championship game that season. Jed's arm was never the same, and he was never a pitcher again. He learned to throw sidearm from his position at shortstop. I wonder if I pushed him too hard, if I was the reason his pitching career was cut down before he made it to high school. It is possible to confuse the healthy principle of entering my son's world with the unhealthy habit of trying to force my son into my world—a world where I wanted our team to win. It's the dangerous pitfall of all parent-coached youth sports.

As much as Jed loved baseball, golf, and football, there was never any competition for his favorite sport—hockey. My own childhood in Arizona was not about hockey, and Jed's hockey career was certainly not about me living vicarious dreams through him. Hockey was new to me, and it cost a fortune. But hockey was great fun for us as a family, and especially for Jed.

For years I was the assistant coach, behind the bench with the primary responsibility of opening and closing the door as the players came on and off the ice. At practices I served the invaluable function of chasing loose pucks or helping the wounded to the bench. If I had been a better player, I would have loved to be a head coach, but I didn't deserve it. You shouldn't expect kids to respect a coach who can't skate as well as they can—when they're eight.

Jed was fluid all over the ice with tremendous hands and great hockey instincts, and true to his character he gladly played wherever his coaches asked him to play. Hockey is a sport that demands ridiculous commitment of both time and resources. Practices, games, tournaments, and travel will take as much of your time as you're willing to give. For us it was always a lot of fun, and Jed played the sport for the love of it. We drew the line and said no to the more demanding schedules of the travel or international teams. We still had a lot of hockey in our lives, and Jed was able to develop into a fine player.

For us sports were a scheduled way to share life together as father and son. Sports were an arena where Jed learned to interact with other people, to connect success with hard work, and to forge sportsmanship and character.

> **SPORTS EXPERIENCES CAN BE A NET POSITIVE OR NEGATIVE, BUT FOR US THEY HAVE BEEN A BLESSING. THEY GAVE ME A NATURAL ENTRY POINT INTO MY SON'S WORLD AND INTO OUR COMMUNITY.**

Sports experiences can be a net positive or negative, but for us they have been a blessing. They gave me a natural entry point into my son's world and into our community. I was always happy to talk with Jed about his games after they were over, but never insistent. I would make observations about his effort or performance, but I was careful not to be critical. When he did well I applauded his effort, or I told him that I could see the difference all his hard work was making. I did *not* equate how much I loved him to how he performed on the field or on the ice. My job as a father was to be encouraging, supportive, present, and interested. When I was a coach my job was to build character and skill with the boys on my team. We had many wonderful times together because we never made it more or less than what it was.

Dad, remember, your son's athletic success is not a reflection of your toughness or athletic prowess. Please, *please* don't be an overbearing ogre. If you find yourself yelling at your boy in the car because of his performance, stop it! You are not helping. Sports are helpful because they teach us how to win and how to lose. Sportsmanship and graciousness are important life traits. Sometimes sports are not fair, but neither is life. Your son will not be world champion; sooner or later there is always some other kid who comes along who is better. But your son can and will grow as he learns to improve. And when the victories and successes do come they can be a whole lot of fun. There is nothing wrong with a little competition; just keep it all in perspective.

ANYTHING WE CAN SHARE IS GOOD.

If your son enjoys sports, then you should attempt to enjoy them as well. As my grandfather used to say, "If it's important to you, then it's important to me." Anything we can share is good.

JED'S SIDE OF THE STORY

I remember joining a T-ball team when I was five years old, but I can't remember when my Dad first started teaching me to throw. I think I was about six months old. So by the time I started as a T-ball player, I could already throw and catch and swing a bat. We were pulling up to practice one afternoon and some of my teammates were on the field already. There was one kid on our team who had a blue glove who was not a very good thrower. I said, "You know, Dad"—because I saw the boy's blue glove in the distance—"that guy with the blue glove, that kid is not very good." I thought I was just being honest.

And my dad looked at me and said something along the lines of, "Jed, you don't talk about your teammates like that." I remember feeling really bad about myself and about the way I had talked cruelly about my teammate. So I refused to do that ever again.

I played sports pretty much all the time growing up. If I wasn't at school, I was at practice. If I wasn't at practice, I was at home playing sports with my friends. If I wasn't playing sports with my friends at home, I was playing sports in video game form with my friends. And if we weren't playing those, I was watching sports with my dad. Or we were eating.

Was it the best way to spend all my time? Not necessarily. If my family had owned a farm and we had spent our time working in the field together, we probably would have been more productive. It might have been good to have more memories of doing service with my family or of knowing the Lord together in prayer.

So even though there are certain things that may have been better, I don't think that participating in sports was wrong. It could have been. With the amount of sporting activity that we did, it could have been really bad. But it was never our god. It was allowed to be what it was, which was an opportunity for living together and joining in fellowship with one another and having fun while we worked hard.

> **BEING ACTIVE AND BEING OUTDOORS IS GOOD, ESPECIALLY WHEN IT IS WITH YOUR DAD.**

Being active and being outdoors is good, especially when it is with your dad. The golf course and the baseball field offered us good opportunities to get to know each other. And teams were important for me with other relationships as well. Being on teams was a good introduction to the world for me. It enabled me to experience life with an array of people, which allowed me to grow in relationships and grow in my ability to handle adversity and to develop some sort of work ethic. In the context of sports, I learned that bonding is good—that being close with people is good.

When my grandpa talks about his experience as a pastor, he spends a lot of time recalling the people he cared for and how he walked with people through hardships and friendships. But he realizes that had he not been titled "pastor," where people were coming to him, he probably would not have done much in regard to participating in his community. His demeanor would have kept him naturally at home and doing his own thing most often, even though he would have enjoyed seeing the friends he came across every once in a while. My demeanor is like Grandpa's: If left alone, I am perfectly content—even if I'm just sitting comfortably in a house. Most of the activities I really enjoyed weren't even things I felt like doing until I got in the middle of them. I didn't even want to go on ski trips half the time—until I started sliding down the mountain. So it does take a little bit of a push to get me to do something, but then when I'm doing that thing, I absolutely adore it and do the best that I can at it. Dad definitely had to push me to get into athletics, and I'm really glad he did.

> **MOST OF THE ACTIVITIES I REALLY ENJOYED WEREN'T EVEN THINGS I FELT LIKE DOING UNTIL I GOT IN THE MIDDLE OF THEM.**

I think without having sports in my life and in my dad's life, I wouldn't be nearly as close with him as I am. I can think more easily now—more quickly and more confidently. And I have a greater confidence level. I can feel comfortable in more settings. Because I played sports, I was forced into all sorts of communities and subcultures, and I was able to understand that even when people are categorized by groups they aren't trapped by them. People are people—in every setting—and I found that rather than being intimidated by them, I could enjoy their company.

PRACTICING PRINCIPLES

*Principle #3: Enter your son's world,
and include him in yours.*

Are you comfortable in your son's world? Have you made conscious efforts to understand his daily environment? How many activities do you regularly share? Would it improve your relationship if you included him in more of your activities?

CHAPTER 4
IT'S UP TO YOU TO TEACH HIM

Principle #4: Train a child in the way he should go.

THE BABY COMES HOME

Who can be prepared for fatherhood? Not me. Sure, when my wife was pregnant I did accompany *her* to Lamaze classes. How nice of me. Lamaze classes, I figured, were there to help her know how to give birth—or be a mother. Same thing.

Was I the only twenty-something guy who was somehow surprised that the day after the baby was born, the day after all the friends and relatives had taken their pictures and left, that we were obliged to take the wiggly little thing home?

I almost said, "Wow, honey! Great job. It's a boy. Hey, you free tonight? Wanna catch a flick?"

But being caught off guard is no excuse. It is like planning the wedding and forgetting the marriage. Fatherhood is upon you—seize the day! And if you are starting out life with a boy, then you have automatically moved into the number one slot in his life in the category of role model. Will he learn to be thoughtful of others? He will if you teach and model thoughtfulness. Will he learn to be physical and expend his energy with healthy and vigorous play? He will if you play with him, encourage him, and let him explore. Will he grow up with an understanding and respect for God? Absolutely—if you teach him that Jesus loves children and always bids them to come to Him.

Now you may feel a little underutilized in the infancy stage of this whole thing. Most men are a little klutzy with the baby. Since men are no good at breast-feeding I think we sometimes reason that our parenting doesn't really begin until the boy joins his first Little League team.

Let's face it, women do most of the heavy lifting in the infancy stage—and I don't care how "Mr. Mom" you were.

Breast-feeding—her territory.

Late-night crying babies—mostly her territory.

Fevers, runny noses, funny coughs—she's on the Internet.

It seems so natural for women, like they just know how to raise babies by instinct. They were made for this, right? I mean, we men do change the occasional dirty diaper, but let's face it—Mom is really in charge.

If you've ever felt this way I have two pieces of advice.

1. Be there, more than ever, for your wife.

Your wife is going to be distracted. This is natural. It is very likely that you will be moved to the back of the line for a while, and this may make you feel somewhat neglected. Fight through this. Man up and serve! There is never going to be a better time for you to step up and be a great guy. Pick up clutter in the house, do the dishes, wash *her* car, call her or text her during the day, and—I'm not kidding—bring her flowers! Men, you can do all you can to help out with the baby but at this stage you need to help out more with your wife. If you do, then I promise you, she'll be back. This little baby that literally came out of her body is going to demand some of her emotional capacity, and it's appropriate. This is no time for you to start feeling needy. So, take lots of pictures. Praise her often, change the diapers, and take joy in your child—but serve your baby by serving your spouse first.

2. Start praying out loud at home.

Your wife wants and needs to see you taking a leadership role in the spiritual development of your family. You can take the reins of this right now by establishing every night prayers with your children as you tuck them in bed. Doesn't matter if they can't speak yet—pray with and over them every day. Also, pray with your wife and ask for God's presence with her every day she mothers, and for God's blessing on your children.

Guys, you do these two things and you'll be serving your young baby very well. Of course, it also doesn't hurt to become a pro at diaper changing.

THE BIRDS, THE BEES, AND THE BIBLE

I'm going to jump ahead here. Let's say you make it through the infant stage, you enjoy the delightful toddler years, you wave good-bye on the first day of kindergarten, you walk the neighborhood in Halloween costumes, you strap up the car seats and drive away for summer vacations, and before you know it your boy is in double digits. He's ten years old! Man, they grow up fast. If your son is in the double digits then it is time for you to really up your game. Dads, you've got the next five or six years to make an indelible imprint on your son's worldview—don't waste your chance.

> **MY REAL QUESTION IS, ARE YOU NOW READY TO DO MORE THAN BE A SPECTATOR? ARE YOU READY TO STEP UP AND LEAD YOUR BOY INTO MANHOOD?**

Lots of dads will invest the quality time attending Little League games, piano recitals, school band concerts, and Cub Scouts gatherings. Great. Congratulations. Here's a medal. My real question is, are you now ready to do more than be a spectator? Are you ready to step up and lead your boy into manhood? These are the years where you can teach him how to do things you know how to do. Do you know how to fix an engine? Teach him how to do it. Do you know how to hit a golf ball? Frame a window? Clean a fish? Serve the poor? Take him with you and teach.

One thing I know all of you know how to do is have sex. You have a kid after all. Yes, you do need to teach your son about sex and sexuality. It is your job and nobody else's. Don't leave this one to the public school health teacher or the older boys on the playground.

Are you ready to sit your son down, look him square in the eye, and talk to him about this? As he starts to become as attracted to the female form as you are, is he going to have an understanding about why he has those feelings and how God intends for him to channel them?

I will admit that when it came to having this talk with our daughter, my wife took the job. Many families do not divide this job up by gender—and I respect that. You and your wife have got to be on the same page for this. My wife spent time with our daughter and they had a wonderful and meaningful time. I had the *privilege* of handling this issue with my son. Here's how it went for us.

The first thing we had to figure out was timing. I was afraid that if I ventured forth too early, it would be a big waste of time.

A six-year-old boy probably hasn't felt anything special when he's looked at the girl across from him in first grade. She doesn't have any shape yet. But if I procrastinated, I could have easily been in danger of waiting too long. By the time the boy is six foot three and a sophomore in high school, I might as well admit I have nothing to offer. The train will have left the station.

I think, when our sons are somewhere between the ages of ten and twelve, we have to muster up the courage, the information, and the faith to do this. I'll admit that it can be a little intimidating. That is why I think you need a plan, and I recommend a trip.

> **THAT IS WHY I THINK YOU NEED A PLAN, AND I RECOMMEND A TRIP.**

Jed was twelve years old when I scheduled a special weekend trip to Chicago for just him and me. I picked him up on a Friday after school, and we set off to the Windy City. Friday night was all his—we would do whatever he wanted to do. For us that meant pizza at Gino's East in downtown Chicago and then lower box seats at Cellular Field for a White Sox-Tigers game. After that, thanks to Priceline.com®, we stayed at a swanky downtown hotel. Friday was all about fun and enjoying time together.

In exchange, Saturday morning was my time. We had gone over the schedule in advance, but I hadn't told him specifically what Saturday morning was going to be all about. So Saturday morning in our cool Hotel Monaco hotel room, I got out my Bible.

"Jed, you're really growing up, and you are soon becoming a man," I said. "Today I'm going to treat you like a man, and we're going to talk about something that is as awesome as anything God has given us. We're going to learn about love, about sex, and about God's design. Are you okay with us discussing this?"

"Yes."

"Okay—let's start in the book of Genesis where we can learn how God created the world and how He created men and women." I opened the Bible and asked him to read out loud these words:

The Lord God said, "It is not good for the man to be alone. I will make a helper suitable for him." Now the Lord God had formed out of the ground all the wild animals and all the birds in the sky. He brought them to the man to see what he would name them; and whatever the man called each living creature, that was its name. So the man gave names to all the livestock, the birds in the sky and all the wild animals. But for Adam no suitable helper was found. So the Lord God caused the man to fall into a deep sleep; and while he was sleeping, he took one of the man's ribs and then closed up the place with flesh. Then the Lord God made a woman from the rib he had taken out of the man, and he brought her to the man. The man said, "This is now bone of my bones and flesh of my flesh; she shall be called 'woman,' for she was taken out of man." For this reason a man will leave his father and mother and be united to his wife, and they will become one flesh. The man and his wife were both naked, and they felt no shame (Genesis 2:18-25 TNIV).

I said a prayer and I asked God to reveal to us His perfect will for men and women and to bless our time together. Then I showed Jed how it all worked. I brought diagrams, charts, pictures—the works. I explained to him how a woman's body had eggs in her uterus, how all the eggs she would ever have in her whole life were in her from the start. I explained how each egg held the potential for new life if it was fertilized by a sperm from a man, and I showed him how the sperm and the egg found each other.

We spent the entire morning in serious, honest, comfortable discussion. It was technical, it was accurate, and it was an understanding of sexuality that a boy needs to learn from the Bible and from his father, if possible.

By noon I was finished. Jed had listened well, and I had only bargained for his time till noon. I packed up the diagrams and books and that was that. I left it alone for a while. We got cleaned up and headed out for an afternoon of fun. We walked downtown and ended up at the ESPN Zone where we ate food and played a whole bunch of video games.

We had a great time. Then in the late afternoon we got back in the car to drive home.

It was his job during the three-hour road trip to repeat back to me the essence of what we had talked about in the morning. I needed to know that he had been listening, that he understood, and that he remembered. He did it all flawlessly.

> **I THINK THAT BY TREATING HIM LIKE A MAN, HE ACTED LIKE ONE.**

He had really been paying attention that morning. He was dialed in. I think that by treating him like a man, he acted like one. Focused and free from distraction, he was more than able to absorb everything I had taught him.

After he finished talking, I asked him the question I had been wondering about all weekend. I didn't know the answer to this question, and I didn't know if he would answer me honestly.

"Jed, how much of this stuff did you already know?"

He shook his head. "Dad, I didn't really know any of it."

Wow. I was relieved. Today parents are raising kids in a whole new world. Kids are exposed to all kinds of sexual material earlier than ever. Jed was twelve years old in 2002. The computer in our house didn't yet have instant access to the kinds of sex acts and pornography that computers have today. Today you had better put filters and protections on every computer in your house if you want to be the one to teach your son about sexuality.

> **TODAY PARENTS ARE RAISING KIDS IN A WHOLE NEW WORLD.**

For Jed and me, the experience was positive and meaningful. It bonded the two of us together in a strong way. But, unfortunately, I checked it off the list, said a big "Amen," and filed it in the "done" category of my life. I probably should have filed it in the "step one completed" category, for I never again had an open and frank talk about sexuality, God's will, and a man's behavior with my son. That omission was a mistake.

A young man is full of testosterone and that means he is chemically wired to think about sex approximately every .18 seconds. This doesn't make him a pervert, nor does it mean he is any different than you were as a teenager. Self-control is one of the fruits of the Holy Spirit, and self-control in the arena of sexuality has never been easy for anyone at any time throughout all of history.

Four years later, when Jed was sixteen, we set out for another father/son ski trip. We bought plane tickets to Utah. Salt Lake City is about as close to major ski slopes as any airport and we were trying to squeeze as much time on the mountains as we could over a three-day weekend. We bought lift tickets for Park City one day and Solitude the next. We only had two days, but they promised to be two great days in light snow, steep slopes, and cold air.

At that time, Jed was a sophomore in high school. Our relationship seemed pretty good to me. I had been traveling more than usual that year and had produced video programs in China, Turkey, Israel, England, and France. So, of course, I had been gone a bit more than usual. I missed a few baseball games in the summer, a couple of golf matches in the fall, and one or two hockey games in the winter—but I was still there for most of his stuff. Since he was now playing on high school teams, I was no longer involved as a coach. I wasn't aware of it at the time, but the drift between us had begun. I was far less in touch with my son than I had assumed. His music was a clue.

> **I WAS FAR LESS IN TOUCH WITH MY SON THAN I HAD ASSUMED. HIS MUSIC WAS A CLUE.**

I always considered myself a pretty cool dad. I own a bunch of guitars and amplifiers, and I play rock-n-roll music a lot so, you know, I must be cool. Certainly I wasn't going to be as far removed from my son's musical tastes as my parents had been from mine. My folks didn't listen to my music, understand it, or ever even express much interest in what I was listening to when I was sixteen years old. I don't think my dad knew the difference between the Doobie Brothers and the Andrews Sisters. But that was him—not me. *I'm cool.*

In the year 2006 the music industry was right in the middle of a seismic shift that would change the business forever. Napster was legal and iPods were taking over the world. Music was more portable and sharable than ever. In my childhood I had to actually save some money, go to a store, and then lay down twelve to fourteen dollars to bring home a new album from Styx or Led Zeppelin or Chicago. But Jed and his friends didn't have to do any of that. They just had to download. And they did, by the thousands of songs. Maybe it is something about being a teenage boy; they seem to need music more than oxygen!

Jed didn't care about the sonic fidelity of his downloads, either. This drove me nuts. Some of the bit rates were so low that his songs sounded like they were coming from a tin can hooked up with a string. Jed didn't seem to notice. When I was sixteen we all obsessed over hi-fidelity stereo components, both at home and in our cars. Everybody was striving to assemble their own high tech stereo system: speakers, needles, turntables, equalizers, receivers, pre-amps, and amplifiers.

But Jed's generation could not have cared less about that stuff. They were satisfied with a distorted boom box or a three-dollar pair of earbuds. Since they had access to a seemingly endless supply of music, they could define their own unique personality by the specific recipe of songs they carried on their iPods. And they took their cues far less from the radio and far more from YouTube.

In my generation, everybody pretty much listened to the same music and it was primarily based on songs introduced and driven by FM radio. But Jed's generation found all kinds of music that never made it to the radio. The Internet had leveled the playing field for musicians, and now anyone who could record and encode a song had de facto worldwide distribution. There would never be another Beatles who could dominate the taste of a generation; there was too much diversity.

Getting in the car with Jed inevitably meant his iPod would be playing before the engine even turned over. But since I'm such a *cool dad*, I wasn't going to object to Jed's newfound eclectic music collection. In Utah on that ski trip we had a fair amount of drive time to and from the ski hills. I figured this was a good chance for me to get to know his world a little bit, listen to his tunes, let him be master of the car stereo.

I said, "Let's hear what you've got. Put your iPod on shuffle, and I'll see if I can name that tune in three notes."

I didn't name many tunes in any number of notes. I was caught off guard. His music was really dark and heavy! I wasn't nearly as cool as I thought. Death and anger were the prevalent themes, not only in the lyrics of songs, but also in the names of half the bands. Some of the singers sounded like they were trying to literally scream their lungs out. Some of the singers apparently died because their lungs came out of their mouths during the reprise. The speed metal bands were firing off so many notes per minute that the guitars sounded more like machine guns than the great tools of rock textures that I understood them to be.

I'm embarrassing myself here by admitting all this, and I know that it takes some pretty amazing skill to maintain a scream for an entire hour-and-a-half show or rip guitar scales at the speed of light, but was this music? These guys made Eddie Van Halen and David Lee Roth seem like the Lawrence Welk Singers.

Parents for many generations have learned the hard way that to question their kids' music is a conversational non-starter. Suddenly I could hear my own Grandma's voice ringing in my ears, "Johnny, why don't you ever listen to some *good* music?" Arrgh. I had become my grandmother! Some of this music was painful. But then, thankfully, the iPod shuffle would engage and something new would come on. Like gangsta rap.

ARRGH. I HAD BECOME MY GRANDMOTHER!

My time with Jed in Utah that year didn't turn out to be the sweet spiritual high that I was anticipating. Maybe it was because the trip was shorter; maybe it was because I wasn't walking as deeply in God's Word as I should have been. I recognized that there was a disconnect unlike anything I'd experienced up until that time in my relationship with my son. When I got back home I said to my wife, "Yeah, the trip was okay, but honestly, I'm not sure I really *enjoy* hanging out with that kid so much anymore."

For the first time I had a taste of the distance many parents experience when their kids wander from home, wander from the faith, or even wander from communication. Some of the most devoted Christian people I knew were grieving over the chasm between themselves and their kids. In many cases that chasm emerged right as their sons turned fifteen, sixteen, or seventeen years old. At fifteen I realized that I didn't know my son as well as I thought I knew him. It was a good time to remember the Scripture that says:

> *Train up a child in the way he should go, and when he is old he will not depart from it* (Proverbs 22:6 NKJV).

BASIC TRAINING

I am reminded that as fathers we are expected to *train* up our children, not just *hope* them up or *expect* them up. Here's a few training tips:

1. Be clear about expectations and consequences, both positive and negative.
2. Open the Bible at home, and find creative excuses to read it out loud.
3. Find out about youth camps, ministries, and retreats and make sure your kids are signed up.
4. Join a local church where the whole family can get *involved*!
5. Listen a lot.
6. Model and expect thoughtfulness.
7. Don't react in anger, ever. Respond appropriately.
8. Be a united front with your wife in all kid-related decisions.
9. Honor their mother.

I trained for a marathon once, and I was able to run it. Okay—it was a half marathon, but I had trained hard and I finished the race with a strong kick and plenty left in the tank. Today even if I were sincerely motivated this afternoon to go outside and run a half marathon, I haven't been training and I wouldn't stand a chance. It wouldn't be enough to just want to do it; I'd have to train for it. A central part of parental training is consistent time spent reading the Bible. It's the training that gives you a foundation from which to parent and from which to lead. Plus, as an added bonus, the Bible is really, really interesting!

> **PLUS, AS AN ADDED BONUS, THE BIBLE IS REALLY, REALLY INTERESTING!**

Lately, I've been attending the local chapter of a Bible Study Fellowship men's group in my hometown. It is encouraging to see more than 400 men get together every Monday night to worship God, meet in small groups to discuss biblical questions, and then gather for a forty-five minute lecture that is straightforward biblical teaching. This fellowship has helped me with the discipline of consistent Bible reading and prayer. But equally impressive to me is that there is a concurrent children's ministry that goes on in the church basement while we are in the meetings. I wish I had exposed my kids to that kind of nuts and bolts biblical teaching when they were young.

I underestimated the ability of young children to trust and comprehend the closeness of God. Jesus said the adults must be more like the kids to inherit the kingdom of heaven; He didn't say the kids needed to be more like the adults! The most powerful life lessons we teach our kids come from the authentic example of how they see us living our lives, not just the words we espouse. We have to show our kids, by example, that the Word of God is relevant in our lives. We have to find creative and engaging ways to pass along the stories, prophecies, teachings, and poems of the Bible to our kids. We should try to surround ourselves with people who love God and are actively engaged in His Word.

> **THE MOST POWERFUL LIFE LESSONS WE TEACH OUR KIDS COME FROM THE AUTHENTIC EXAMPLE OF HOW THEY SEE US LIVING OUR LIVES.**

This doesn't mean we should force our kids to sit through endless services at churches that are boring, passionless, or watered-down. There are groups that are sharing authentic Christian lives out there—camps, churches, conferences, communities, or concerts where there is a passion for God, a deep respect for the text, and a dynamic hunger for the Holy Spirit. Those are the places where your kids will truly be engaged and introduced to God.

But in addition to all these things, it is vital that your son observes that the Bible is open in your home, in your car, and within the context of real life. I didn't want church to be the only place my kids ever saw me opening the Bible. If you don't open the Bible in front of your kids, you are depriving them of an opportunity to discover God. That doesn't mean you force it on kids like broccoli or spinach: "Eat this! It's good for you!" The Bible isn't broccoli; it's more like a smorgasbord of everything great under the sun. So prepare the meals in meal-size portions, with tasty recipes, drawing from the entire menu.

I've recently released a series of videos called "Watch & Talk," presented by Rebecca St. James. They are short films that are designed to instigate simple and fun home family Bible studies. If you are interested in trying this with your kids, check out www.watch-n-talk.com.

Does that mean your teenagers will automatically become deep students of the Scriptures, voraciously devouring book after book, studying, learning, internalizing, and applying God's Word? I hope so, but probably not. But you are sowing seeds and I believe the Word of God will work in ways we cannot even see.

A short time after our ski trip to Utah, I had a talk with Jed. I asked him how his walk with the Lord was going.

"My belief is pretty good," he replied. "My walk, not so much."

I challenged him to open his Bible more, to read it on his own time and on his own initiative. At that point in his life I think he heard me, but he wasn't really listening.

A foolish son is grief to his father and bitterness to the one who bore him (Proverbs 17:25 HCSB).

JED'S SIDE OF THE STORY

When I was little I listened to the music my parents always listened to, and that was good. And eventually I heard some other music that my friends had, and that was pretty good. And then I heard a little bit heavier music, and that was cooler. The more intense it was, the cooler it was. Eventually I reached a point where, in order for me to get pumped about a song, it had to be heavier than the one before. And as the music got heavier, I didn't even notice myself slowly becoming angrier than I was before. So I would continue to listen to heavier and heavier stuff until I reached a point where I hit a wall. It was as heavy and as dark as it could get, and suddenly I realized that I was way past the decision I'd made long before about what I was going to allow myself to listen to.

Middle school was hard. Dad warned me that it would be some of the hardest years, and he was right. I knew they were hard in the midst of them—the most difficult socially—and I knew I was lonely. It was like being in a boat on water and not knowing where I was or where the waves would take me, so I just kind of held on to the boat. I was pretty sure that my boat would be okay eventually, and I just kind of moved around, but I didn't take any control of where it was going. My friends were in the same situation that I was. We didn't know where we were going or what was going on—we were just along for the ride.

> **I WAS ENTRENCHED IN A WORLD I HADN'T PLANNED ON BEING A PART OF.**

My dad wrote that the adolescent years are a critical time for parents to pay attention and to stay involved in the specifics of their kids' lives. Looking back on it, I believe that is absolutely true because I don't even know how I got to the places I got to. It wasn't anything to do with my reasoning or planning. I was just given over to the influence of my world. My world shaped who I would become, and so by the time I was a sophomore in high school, I was entrenched in a world I hadn't planned on being a part of.

A SLOW SLIDE

The journey into pornography was similar to the one that took me into dark music. I didn't even notice what was happening at the start. I didn't even think it was bad. I had learned about sex, but we'd never talked about pornography or masturbation or stuff like that. And so even though I probably would have conceded that they were not of God and that I shouldn't do them, I was never really taught that from an authority until it was a little too late. By the time I heard it, I'd already seen too much. I never had sex because I had set that barrier, but I hadn't really understood forms of purity beyond that. And I just ended up in a stuck place. I was constantly questioning myself, what other people said, and what Scripture said—and I was lost. I was afraid, even. Everything I didn't understand I became afraid of, which is what happens when your sinful desires take over.

> **I WAS CONSTANTLY QUESTIONING MYSELF, WHAT OTHER PEOPLE SAID, AND WHAT SCRIPTURE SAID—AND I WAS LOST.**

When I was a kid, I thought that as long as I was a little bit better than the people around me, then I was still okay in the eyes of God. If my friends were looking at junk and I averted my eyes *mostly*, I felt like I was doing pretty well. The concept of holiness, a godly holiness, was something I hadn't grasped. I hadn't grasped that we're judged not in a hierarchy with each other, but according to Christ and His person.

More than that, I really didn't know God. I didn't know the Holy Spirit. So it was easy for me to fall into temptation. There wasn't one time where I decided "Okay, I'm just gonna become a sinner now because this is better." Instead I just consistently allowed myself to believe the lie that something dark was actually not so dark.

> **I CONSISTENTLY ALLOWED MYSELF TO BELIEVE THE LIE THAT SOMETHING DARK WAS ACTUALLY NOT SO DARK.**

I think I probably would have been very easily stopped if anyone had known, anyone beyond a friend who was struggling just as badly as me. If a parent had known, I probably would've just cried for a while and asked for help and then gotten out. Even when I was into pornography just a little bit, I despised it just as much as I liked it. It's a tender thing because, at that age, parents know their kids are pretty rebellious. The kids act like they don't want to hear anything their parents have to say. But in actuality, the Word of God is really freeing, and I would have wanted freedom.

A lot of the things that are taboo or are awkward or funny for kids to talk about are just things that haven't been talked about. Since they haven't been talked about, everyone feels like they'll be bad to discuss. But that's not true.

I took a trip to Israel the summer after my sophomore year in college with the great Bible teacher Ray Vander Laan. Near Jerusalem, we visited the ruins of ancient homes that had been filled with multiple generations of extended family in one shared space. Someone asked the question, "If everyone's living so close to each other all the time, where do the husbands and wives sleep together?" The answer was that the families had one room specifically designated for marital relations. Couples would plan ahead and then tell everyone when they were going to need their space.

It's Up to You to Teach Him

In other words, marriage and romance don't have to be taboo subjects. When it's something that's known and understood, sexuality can be great and exciting and God-honoring. It doesn't have to be a secret. And when parents can talk about it in that way, their children won't be left alone with temptations they don't know what to do with.

> **UNDERSTAND THAT IF YOUR KID DOESN'T HAVE EARS TO HEAR, YOU'RE NOT GOING TO BE ABLE TO PRY THEM OPEN WITH YOUR BARE HANDS.**

I encourage parents to be open with their kids and to talk with them. Teach them the Scriptures and don't be afraid of uncomfortable topics. Be patient and be careful about timing. Understand that if your kid doesn't have ears to hear, you're not going to be able to pry them open with your bare hands. But that doesn't need to stop you from speaking the Word of the Lord to them and letting the Word do what the Word does. Continue to pray. Immerse your family in the family of Christ. And if you're doing your part, you can trust the Holy Spirit to handle the heart.

PRACTICING PRINCIPLES

Principle #4: Train a child in the way he should go.

Have you moved from the spectator to the teacher role in your children's lives? Did this chapter make you think more seriously about your role in providing biblical answers to important aspects of teenage life including sex and music? Are you trusting the Holy Spirit to guide you?

CHAPTER 5
SHARING THE LOAD

*Principle #5: Focus on three essentials:
a legacy, a community, and a mentor.*

In August 2006, our family underwent a radical change. There was no way to prepare for it; there was no avoiding it. It was not a bad thing, but it completely altered the rhythm and balance of our family. Our daughter moved out.

Of course, it was expected. After all, she graduated from high school and had been accepted to college, so I suppose I shouldn't have been so surprised. But who is really prepared emotionally for any of the big changes of life. I don't know that you *can* prepare. These are our frontiers.

Our daughter Jordyn is seventeen months older and two years in school ahead of her brother. She did very well in school academically, athletically, and socially. She managed to earn her own 4.0 GPA and make varsity teams in volleyball and tennis, but it was always clear that achievements were never what really motivated Jordyn. She was first chair violin in the school orchestra, but she would gladly yield the position simply because the second chair violinist wanted it more than she did. She took her academics seriously, but never considered herself a scholar. She performed great in sports, but always assumed she wouldn't make the team.

Her senior year she was lined up to be the starting setter on the varsity volleyball team and very likely a team captain. The season promised to be a grand culmination of years of travel, hard work, and persistence. But to my surprise she decided something else was more important than varsity volleyball.

She had been volunteering with a student ministry organization called Young Life, specifically with their junior high branch called Wyldlife. She was also serving as a student mentor and advisor through a school program called PALS. Jordyn loved spending time with younger kids and she took her volunteer ministry jobs seriously—so seriously, in fact, that when she looked at how much time she was going to have to put into varsity volleyball, she decided it was no longer worth the time invested. She started asking herself these questions: Who am I after all the things that I do are taken away? Who am I in relation to God? Am I content to be defined as a volleyball player, a violinist, a tennis player, a piano player, and a student?

She "retired" from volleyball right before her senior season, right on the brink of her chance at stardom. Being a star just didn't matter to her as much as the chance to help other people and pour into them.

Her rearranged priorities taught me a lot. A year later she was off to college at Point Loma Nazarene University, a school that sits along the beautiful coastline of the Pacific Ocean in San Diego, California. I think that school was geographically as far from Michigan as one could get within in the Continental USA.

For the next two years Jed lived at home, a de facto only child—except that he always had friends over. Always. We converted our living room into a game room. Judy put food out every night for whoever happened to be around. Jed hosted study groups, sports groups, driveway hockey games, and more. On any given night there were between three and eight guys living out of the house.

> **WE CONVERTED OUR LIVING ROOM INTO A GAME ROOM. JUDY PUT FOOD OUT EVERY NIGHT FOR WHOEVER HAPPENED TO BE AROUND.**

For a year and a half our house also became the gathering place of a small Christian student movement known as the Ancient Roots Community or ARC. The ARC groups had one central aim—seek God and do whatever He said to do. They would sing and worship, pray, and seek God. No chaperone required.

As ARC groups started meeting regularly in our basement, more and more our house really did become a house of prayer. This seemed like a good thing to me. Our house—a house of prayer—and not because of Judy or me but because of Jed and his friends. How cool is that?

In high school Jed had this quality that made other guys want to hang around with him. He was genuine, he was funny, he legitimately liked people, and he wasn't emotionally needy. He was good friends with the close-knit group of guys he played hockey with, and he was equally at ease with the rough and rugged group of guys from the baseball team. In the non-jock world, Jed regularly used our dining room to host study groups for the AP physics, chemistry, and mathematics geeks in his school. At the same time, Jed hung around with ROTC kids, golf team kids, outgoing popular kids, and shy outcast kids. They all seemed to like Jed, and he was friends with them all—even those who knew he wasn't going to party with them. From ARC worship groups to baseball "dirtbags"—that's a wide swatch of friends, no matter how you look at it.

It was this quality that made me want to put Jed on the screen for the film, *The Frontier Boys*. Winsome movie stars have an indescribable quality that simply attracts people to them. They draw people to themselves because of something—it could be their physical attractiveness, their confidence, their unique talent, or some special giftedness. It's a hard-to-define quality, but you know it when you see it. Whatever that quality is, Jed had it.

BUT HOW DID HE GET TO JESUS?

By his senior year of high school, Jed's walk with God had become much more personal for him. But what had triggered the switch and when did it happen? Something had brought him out of the funk he had been in two years earlier; something had transformed him into a kid who was hosting student-led worship groups in our basement. That something was a someone—Jesus. But how did he get to Jesus? There were three things that I believe made a big difference: a legacy, a community, and a mentor.

A LEGACY

Every young man wants to know who he is and where he comes from, but many boys today know very little of their own ancestry or heritage.

The Bible speaks of the great benefit of a godly legacy.

> *...Blessed is the man who fears the Lord, who delights greatly in His commandments. His descendants will be mighty on earth; the generation of the upright will be blessed* (Psalm 112:1-2 NKJV).

> *His mercy extends to those who fear him, from generation to generation* (Luke 1:50).

> *...I, the Lord your God, am a jealous God, punishing the children for the fathers' sin to the third and fourth generations of those who hate Me, but showing faithful love to a thousand*

generations of those who love Me and keep My commands (Deuteronomy 5:9-10 HCSB).

Both of Jed's grandfathers were pastors who had well-respected careers in ministry. Jed's heritage is one of faith; he happens to come from a legacy of men who claimed Christ. So even when he wasn't acting like it, Jed knew who he was. Every father has the opportunity to extend or initiate that legacy of faith for his son. God says He will show His love to a *thousand* generations of those who love Him and keep His commandments!

> **WHEN A FATHER STANDS UP FOR CHRIST IN FRONT OF HIS KIDS AND MAKES IT KNOWN THAT HE LOVES GOD AND STRIVES TO KEEP HIS COMMANDMENTS, THAT MAN IS SURELY CHANGING THE WORLD.**

When a father stands up for Christ in front of his kids and makes it known that he loves God and strives to keep His commandments, that man is surely changing the world. Even if he doesn't accomplish anything spectacular in the eyes of the world he's done something eternal in the lives of his children. As a father I believed it was essential for me to extend the legacy of faith that was passed down to me.

A COMMUNITY

Parents' impact on their kids' faith is huge, but it has limitations. Parents' voices can become easy for kids to dismiss, and sooner or later most kids will question their parents in some way. That's why the community is so vital in raising kids. Your adult friends will have a tremendous influence on your kids, so choose your friends wisely. My wife and I cultivate long-term relationships with people who love the Lord and who have shown an interest in our kids. Because of that community, Jed was usually among adults of faith. My good friend Bruce Snoap, who has been the sound man for Grooters & Beal for years and who was an associate producer for *The Frontier Boys*, has known and cared for Jed since the day he was born. Bruce made sure both my kids knew that anywhere, anytime they ever needed anything, he was just a phone call away.

> **MY WIFE AND I CULTIVATE LONG-TERM RELATIONSHIPS WITH PEOPLE WHO LOVE THE LORD AND WHO HAVE SHOWN AN INTEREST IN OUR KIDS.**

When Jed was ten years old, we bought him a Yamaha drum kit and signed him up for lessons with my good friend Danny Reyes. The fact that Danny is a world-class drummer and musician was nice; the fact that Danny was another godly man and influence in Jed's life was critical.

I brought Jed with me when I attended an arts and worship conference in the Netherlands because I wanted him to meet other men of faith who were planting and serving churches in Europe. It was important that Jed see firsthand that there were faithful followers of Jesus all over the world, even in post-Christian Amsterdam!

Our community is the big "C" church—the family of God who is scattered all over the globe. My son has known from day one that he belonged within this community and that this community loved him and knew him.

I learned that even if I was the most dedicated father in the world, it was not enough. My son needed other voices in his life that invested in him, affirmed him, and challenged him in ways I couldn't. Look around; find such people. Enlist them. Make sure your social life includes time for these people to hang around your kids.

A SPIRITUAL MENTOR

Every man needs a key spiritual mentor at some point in his life. A spiritual mentor is that person who comes alongside a person and inspires him to go places he didn't even know he *could* go. A mentor unlocks his potential.

When I was twelve years old I had a mentor named Larry Anderson. Larry was cool; he played football, he played guitar, and he lived his life for Jesus. Larry was a Young Life leader. Because of him I signed up for a Young Life Camp the week before I began college. That single week at Windy Gap in South Carolina was a huge turning point for me in my faith and the direction of my life. If not for Larry, I would have never done that week. If not for that week, my whole life would have turned out differently.

When Jed was in high school he met a guy who would become a key spiritual mentor for him. Herb Barbutti was only a few years older than Jed, but he had lived an incredible life by the age of twenty-two. He had traveled the world, taught in mission schools, and worked for Iris Ministries in Mozambique, Africa with missionaries Roland and Heidi Baker. Herb had seen the power of God through many healings and miracles. His walk with God was real and it was passionate. But Herb was always on the move. Whenever he came back to Holland to visit, he always found a way to serve God. He often met people for coffee and encouraged them in their walk with Christ. He would spontaneously drop by the hospital to just visit and pray with sick people—people he didn't know. Herb is an unusual, interesting, and inspiring guy.

> **HE WOULD SPONTANEOUSLY DROP BY THE HOSPITAL TO JUST VISIT AND PRAY WITH SICK PEOPLE—PEOPLE HE DIDN'T KNOW.**

Herb was the founder of the Ancient Roots Communities movement—the group that had been meeting in our basement. His desire was to ignite a passion for God in the hearts of his generation. Two of the hearts he touched were our two kids. Herb's easy smile and infectious spirit have helped lead many people into the presence of the Holy Spirit.

As I write this, Herb and his young bride are living in Brazil with their newborn baby, ministering in a poor community that is a hotbed of the international sex trafficking industry. They are bringing light to the darkness. Herb's mentorship and discipleship made a difference in Jed in a way that I never could have.

> **THESE YOUNG PEOPLE TAKE THE PROPHECY FOUND IN ISAIAH 61 AS A PERSONAL CALL TO ACTION.**

Now Jed carries a passion for bringing light to the darkness when he and a group of his friends go out every Friday night to do outreach among the homeless and the destitute on the streets, on the beaches, or in the riverbeds of San Diego County. These young people take the prophecy found in Isaiah 61 as a personal call to action:

> *The Spirit of the Sovereign Lord is on me, because the Lord has anointed me to proclaim good news to the poor. He has sent me to bind up the brokenhearted, to proclaim freedom for the captives and release from darkness for the prisoners* (Isaiah 61:1 TNIV).

These kids are part of a generation that does not just declare themselves hungry for Christ; they feed on Him. And they share the bread.

I am part of a generation of Christians who came through college in the '80s. We were inspired by singer Keith Green, challenged by the teachings of Tony Campolo, and invigorated by the evangelist John Guest. Many of the Christians in my generation went on to proclaim and serve Christ through church and mission organizations. Some of us turned to the arts to glorify God. My own company has this mission statement: "To reveal the beauty of Christ to the world through excellent media." But I see a young generation today that takes its obedience to Christ even deeper. They are prepared to lay down their lives for the sake of the cross. They have heard the words of Christ:

> *For whoever wants to save his life will lose it, but whoever loses his life because of Me and the gospel will save it* (Mark 8:35 HCSB).

In return, I've seen that God is filling this generation with the powerful gifts and fruits of the Holy Spirit. They are healing the sick, they are bringing hope to the poor, they are living in community with one another, and they are studying and absorbing the Word of God in deep and relevant ways. I've never seen anything like it before—but I've seen it growing from a small group of kids in the basement of my own house!

So when it came time for Jed to choose a college, his love of hockey took second place to his desire to put himself in the center of a strong community of God. He chose to follow his sister to San Diego and he enrolled in Point Loma Nazarene University. For me his decision meant that if I wanted to watch him play hockey anymore it would have to be in summer men's league. But it also meant that we had two more years of legitimate excuses to visit San Diego, one of the most beautiful cities in America.

> **BE OPEN TO A SPIRITUAL MENTOR IN YOUR SON'S LIFE. IF YOU SEE ONE COME ALONG, DON'T FEEL THREATENED. NO DAD CAN DO IT ALL.**

That is how legacy, community, and spiritual mentorship played out with my son. It is impossible to pick your son's friends as he goes through life, but you are able to open your home to a God-fearing community of friends. You may not have a deep heritage of faith in your own ancestry, but you could seek out men of wisdom and faith and find creative ways for them to interact with your son. Be open to a spiritual mentor in your son's life. If you see one come along, don't feel threatened. No dad can do it all.

JED'S SIDE OF THE STORY

Before I actually grasped that God was real, God had been an important aspect of my life. An "aspect" is a terrible way to describe God. If you're a creature, if you have been made, you are God's. This isn't an option for us to consider; this is the reality. And this isn't something that I knew. I was a Christian in *my* understanding, which meant that I was nice, I didn't swear, and I was convicted that drinking and smoking and having sex before marriage were wrong. I would say Jesus was my Lord, which was very significant, but what that meant for me was that I would go to summer camps and church on Sundays if I felt like it, and when I died, I would go to Heaven.

I never knew of the Holy Spirit other than the words. I never knew that God had called me and made me for a purpose. I never knew that God had sent His Son, not just so that I could claim eternal life in Him later, but so that I would be alive with Him now. I never knew what a privilege it was to pray to and praise Him and that, as I understood the grace of His forgiveness, my only response would be gratitude. I didn't know these things.

> **BECAUSE GOD WAS SIMPLY AN OPTION RATHER THAN THE LIFE AND THE WAY AND THE TRUTH, OTHER OPTIONS HAD A STRONG EFFECT ON ME AS WELL.**

I didn't know that my hands could heal the sick because He was in me. I didn't know that I could speak to people and see them know that the Lord loved them. I didn't know that in giving up my life for people, I would actually find myself.

So because God was simply an option rather than the Life and the Way and the Truth, other options had a strong effect on me as well. In high school, most of my time was spent at school with other adolescent boys, playing sports with adolescent boys, or watching television (sometimes with adolescent boys). There was no doubt that I was going to experience temptation, and it was likely that I would give in to it.

So my eyes and ears ended up plagued—filled with darkness through pornography and through music that advocated hate. And I was a Christian, you could say. But I was depressed, and I was getting angrier. I knew that I despised myself. I knew that I was getting more easily frustrated. I didn't really care much about others. This was the trajectory of my life at the time.

BUT MY SISTER…

My older sister graduated high school early so she could work and save money for college—and pray every day until four in the morning. So there was this noticeable difference in the path of our lives. I was completely oblivious to it at the time, but she continued on this trajectory, being led by Herb Barbutti, who had been told one day by the Spirit of the Lord to call her. So he did, and she learned that God was very real and that He loved her very much. When she was touched by His Spirit, there was little she could do but praise Him and give herself to Him. So she went on pursuing God as I continued to live for pretty immediate pleasures, while still holding on to Jesus—whatever that meant.

> **WHEN SHE WAS TOUCHED BY HIS SPIRIT, THERE WAS LITTLE SHE COULD DO BUT PRAISE HIM AND GIVE HERSELF TO HIM.**

I remember going to an Indian restaurant with my dad and Jordyn and Herb. It was a meeting appropriately called by my father because his daughter, who had always been a pretty good girl, was suddenly staying up all night praying and reading the Bible with a group of people she had never really spent time with before. He wanted to make sure this wasn't a cult or a cover for something else that was actually going on.

Herb is legitimate. And he was honest and open with my dad, not trying to hide anything. He was a guy who had come to know the Lord and knew that God wasn't terribly concerned with him fulfilling the American dream. So before he graduated high school, he went to Africa to be a missionary. There he saw the blind see and thousands get baptized and saved. He told very concrete stories: "This is what we were doing; this is where we went; this is how things happened. This person who was once dead is now alive again."

I was not only completely unaffected by what was spoken, but I legitimately didn't hear these things. It didn't register with me that God actually healed people now or that, if He still did, how it had any significance for me at all. It went in one ear and out the other. I was at that conversation, but I was nowhere near that conversation while we were there. I was looking at Herb, but I wasn't ready to hear him.

So two years later, my senior year, I continued to be involved in all sorts of sin. I wasn't necessarily okay with it, but I wasn't sure what to do with it. I enjoyed my sins more than I would have enjoyed the effort to stop them.

But my sister went to Mozambique for a summer and had more stories. And it was harder to ignore the voice of the one I grew up with, looked up to, followed in the footsteps of, knew everything about—insecurities and all—as she told me with excitement and open eyes and wonder that for some reason God chose to work through her and heal every person she laid hands on for two hours. She had been, and kept on, praying for me for years. I know she wept for me multiple times—which was interesting for her because for a long time she couldn't cry at all. It's hard to ignore that pressing, that witness, that Spirit that comes when someone acts that way.

> **GOD CHOSE TO WORK THROUGH HER AND HEAL EVERY PERSON SHE LAID HANDS ON FOR TWO HOURS.**

So I was in sin, and I knew it, and all of a sudden, I had a counterpart—a sister who said, "You don't have to be in sin. You don't have to be captivated by that. God is good. God is life, and God is fun, and God demands everything that you are, and you won't regret it when you give yourself to Him. You'll find yourself there, and you'll find One who is far greater than you. And you'll find lots of others who have found the One far greater than you."

MAKING THE SWITCH

Around the second half of my senior year, I saw that I was angry and trapped. And I decided that I was going to change my ways and somehow find this Jesus. I knew that if my life was going to belong to Jesus, it couldn't maintain its current habits.

First I started switching the music I listened to. Leeland and Switchfoot were about the only Christian bands I knew. Then I started praying every once in a while. And I couldn't tell you a time or an event that happened necessarily, but by the time summer came around, all I cared about was serving the Lord, praising Him, worshiping Him, reading Scriptures, finding out more about who He is, and being a person of prayer. I was freed from pornography. It was a hard battle and still is a temptation at times, but I was *so* overcome by the joy of the Lord. I cared simply about knowing God—and that was it.

> **I KNEW THAT IF MY LIFE WAS GOING TO BELONG TO JESUS, IT COULDN'T MAINTAIN ITS CURRENT HABITS.**

It was then that I was able to notice the community around me. I had my sister and other brothers and sisters in Christ, who would testify of the things of the Lord that they had seen. I had my parents' friends, who had been loving me for years and from who I was finally able to receive the wisdom and example offered me for my whole life. And I had my family—grandparents who loved the Lord and who had been praying for me daily since I was born. It was a community that had always been there, and I was for the first time realizing the impact of their witness to me. The world I had grown up in simply became a new place.

I came into my senior year expecting to graduate as valedictorian, go to college, and become a doctor or engineer and make a good life for myself while being a Christian. I exited senior year realizing that I was absolutely a heathen—gross and a sinner—who was offered grace over and over until I couldn't resist it anymore. And I exited senior year caring about nothing but witnessing of the God who loves me and who continues to love me, who is very, very strong and very alive.

Then I went to college—looking for a mission field. And I learned in college that I was equipped to witness of the God I knew and that I was also very much still ignorant and immature. God is far more than I knew when I first met Him. And I learned that there is no life other than serving Him. It can look a lot of different ways, but it always looks like Jesus, and it always comes with the Holy Spirit.

PRACTICING PRINCIPLES

*Principle #5: Focus on three essentials:
a legacy, a community, and a mentor.*

Is your legacy one you and your family will be proud of in the years to come? More importantly, is it one that God is proud of today? How committed are you to building a safe and loving community in which your children can learn and grow? Are you willing to become a mentor to those who need your God-given gifts and talents? Are you willing to allow a God-sent mentor into your children's lives?

CHAPTER 6
STEPPING INTO THE WATERS

Principle #6: God's timing is always perfect.

It was early one November morning, hours before the sunrise, and I was sitting at my desk. "God," I prayed, "do You want me to make this film or not?" By this time I had tried just about everything I knew how to do to make *The Frontier Boys* happen. I had written a novel, a screenplay, shot a proof of concept trailer, had traveled to Hollywood and shared the project with studio executives at Sony, Fox, Walden, and Disney. I had hired three different development guys to try and raise private equity investment funds. The net result of all those efforts had been a grand total of zero dollars invested and nary a thread of interest from the studios. So as I prayed I was seriously wondering before God if it was time to give up on this dream.

But I couldn't shake the feeling that it *was* time, and that I was being nudged to move forward and make the film. I prayed earnestly that I would truly discern the voice of God on this issue, not just the voice of my own passions. Then I wrote an email to Jed.

> Hey Jed,
>
> Couldn't sleep this morning. Feeling led to move forward to produce *The Frontier Boys*, but I just can't imagine doing it without you.

Please pray for God's leading.

Love you,

Dad

Jed was in the middle of the fall semester of his sophomore year in college. I didn't see any realistic way we were going to be able to shoot a winter film with no money and with no chance of getting him to a Northern Michigan set for six weeks while he was in school in Southern California. I considered trying to shoot all his scenes during Christmas break—but that never actually made sense within the realities of a film shoot schedule. It was probably time to let go of *The Frontier Boys*, at least as a film. A couple weeks later Judy and I flew to San Diego to spend the Thanksgiving holiday with the kids in a little cottage in Pacific Beach.

Thanksgiving in San Diego is beautiful, but it feels to me a little like cheating. Michigan Thanksgivings mean deserted lakes, light snowfall, and football on wet or frozen brown grass.

But Thanksgiving in San Diego meant turkey dinner on the deck under the umbrella, the roar of the Pacific Ocean as background music, and football on the sand. We made the appropriate emotional adjustments.

As we sat around the picnic table Jed made a surprise announcement.

"I've decided to drop out of college."

"That's nice, could you pass the squash?"

Drop out of college? He was only halfway through college. His GPA was 3.9, he was on a scholarship, and he was having the time of his life. So far everything about his experience in college had been fantastic.

So I asked the obvious question. "Why?"

"Well, I've been praying a lot," Jed said. "I want to spend some time in Kansas City with Herb. And I want to plug in to IHOP (The International House of Prayer). I think God is leading me to do this."

"Is this a temporary thing, or are you thinking this is a permanent decision?"

"I'm not sure. It might be temporary, unless God calls me somewhere else."

My wife was understandably anxious about the idea of dropping out. She had personally experienced how hard it can be to get back into the swing of college once you take a break. When we were in college she suffered a major injury to her knee during a varsity volleyball game. In the early '80s when you tore your ACL your career was basically over. Take it from Billy Sims, the great running back of the Detroit Lions, whose career ended early with that same injury. Judy went into surgery the very next day and came out with a cast that went from her toes to her hip. Three months later, when the cast came off, she was in physical therapy up to six hours a day. The pain and the distractions made it tough to concentrate on schoolwork, so after her freshman year, she dropped out for a while. She eventually went back and finished her degree, but she found out how difficult it was to re-engage with college life once you had left it. She realized that many students who leave college never return. She knew that Jed was gifted academically, and while she didn't question his sincerity, she wondered about his timing. He was only able to attend the school he was attending because of a generous academic scholarship; dropping out would certainly put that at risk, even if he decided to return one day.

> **DROPPING OUT WOULD CERTAINLY PUT THAT AT RISK, EVEN IF HE DECIDED TO RETURN ONE DAY.**

I had a slightly different view; I saw this as an unforeseeable opportunity to have a once-in-a-lifetime chance for us to do something together we never dreamed would be possible. I saw this as a window to produce a film where Jed could be available to act in one of the lead roles.

At that time I wasn't even sure he was interested in doing the film, even if we got the funding to move ahead. Jed's reason for leaving college was to go to Kansas City to get involved in ministry training and discipleship. He saw this time in his life as one of the few when he could be led and mentored on a daily basis, and he wanted to take advantage of the opportunity.

Obviously, it was something he felt very deeply. He was enjoying college, doing great socially and academically, and he had fallen in love with a girl. Jed's first serious girlfriend was in California—the girl he would propose to a year later—and he would be moving to Kansas City where the only way he could see her was through Skype!

And even though this was a window to produce the film that only God could have opened up, I still didn't know if we could proceed. I was eager to move ahead, but we just didn't have the money. I searched the Scriptures and came up with two passages that competed for my thinking throughout the process. One said:

> *For which of you, wanting to build a tower, doesn't first sit down and calculate the cost to see if he has enough to complete it? Otherwise, after he has laid the foundation and cannot finish it, all the onlookers will begin to make fun of him, saying "This man started to build and wasn't able to finish"* (Luke 14:28-30 HCSB).

COUNTING THE COST

This kind of sensible tower-building planning made perfect sense, and so we produced very detailed production budgets. We developed business plans and investment portfolios. We studied other films in the genre and knew which ones had succeeded and which ones had failed. The cost of a tower and the cost of a film are, however, a little like comparing apples and oranges. If you know how high you want to build your tower and you know your labor and materials costs, it's pretty easy to estimate your total building costs. Films, on the other hand, are as unpredictable to budget for as airplane seats. One day an airplane seat costs you $350; the next day the same seat jumps to $750. I don't get it. Production costs for feature films, as most people know, can cost well over $100 million dollars. Or they can cost $50 million dollars. Or they can cost $20 million dollars. Or, if it's a made-for-television film, it might cost $2.4 million dollars. Or if it was shot on the cheap with volunteers and borrowed equipment, it could be put together for $100 thousand dollars. Where did we fit in this spectrum?

How could I be obedient to Jesus' own words telling me to calculate the costs of a tower that could cost anywhere between $100 thousand and $100 million dollars? How much should *The Frontier Boys* cost? How much production value was necessary? We carefully worked out a complete line item budget. We included every detail, from preproduction expenses, office costs, travel and lodging, equipment rentals, location fees, casting costs, actor contracts, crew costs, catering and craft services, legal expenses, insurances, editorial expenses, graphics and special effects, sound design, music composition, song licensing, digital intermediate costs, film prints, promotion and advertising costs, and more. It is a long list. I came to a figure—$2.4 million dollars. I had very specific ideas for what kind of cameras and lenses I wanted to shoot with, and I had high hopes for the quality of actors I wanted to find. I thought if we were especially frugal, and if people would be willing to work for modest pay, we could pull off a film with the production values of a big budget action feature for the bargain low price of $2.4 million. I felt pretty good about that. But we didn't have that kind of money. Actually, we didn't have any money.

ACTUALLY, WE DIDN'T HAVE ANY MONEY.

So we reworked the budget, recalculated every cost. We shaved, cut, compromised, went brutal, but tried to be honest. Could I possibly, conceivably, produce this film for a million dollars less than the budget I had originally worked up? Was there any way to imagine doing this if I only had $1.4 million to spend?

We modified about a thousand line items and printed out a multi-page film budget that dropped our production expenses to $1.4 million. That was as low as I could fathom; that was bare bones. And we'd have to rely on talent, hard work, sweat equity, and the grace of God to make the film I wanted to make for that little. But then, we didn't even have that little.

Shortly after Jed's decision to drop out of school, I made a renewed effort to see if I could build up a team of investors to come behind our project. By that time we had one distributor who had signed a letter of intent based on the trailer, the script, and the business plan. This time I wasn't going to rely on anyone else to help me raise the funds; I was going to do the work myself. I began making phone calls, setting up meetings, and sharing my vision. Finally we got our first investor. A substantial sum of money came in from a wonderful woman from Texas who believed in the vision of the film and believed in me. I was ecstatic. We were on the way.

Now I have one advantage in this deal and that is that my wife and I are owners of a terrific little production company. We have a great group of really talented professionals, and we have the equipment and gear to handle the post-production of a film. We have done it for other feature films. We can do the editorial, the sound design, the color, and the special effects. We have graphic artists who can design posters and programmers who can develop websites. We have the in-house ability to stretch a production dollar thanks to the quality team we have at Grooters Productions.

Partly because of that team, and partly because I was convinced we were being called to move ahead with the film, we prepared one final budget. I knew we would need some money to advertise and promote the film, so I settled on a low, low budget that allotted two-thirds for production of the film and one-third for P&A (Prints and Advertising) and overhead. I wasn't sure if the film I could make for that budget could possibly look as good as I wanted it to or attract the kind of talent I was hoping to work with. Many people would have to compromise their rates; many workers would literally have to volunteer; and a million little things would just have to fall in place. But even then, the truth was, we still didn't have enough money.

That is where the other Scripture came into play.

> *Joshua told the people, "Consecrate yourselves, for tomorrow the Lord will do amazing things among you."…"Tell the priests who carry the ark of the covenant: 'When you reach the edge of the Jordan's waters, go and stand in the river.'" Joshua said to the Israelites, "Come here and listen to the words of the Lord your God. This is how you will know that the living God is among you.…As soon as the priests who carry the ark of the Lord—the Lord of all the earth—set foot in the Jordan, its waters flowing downstream will be cut off and stand up in a heap"* (Joshua 3:5, 8-10, 13).

STEPPING OUT IN FAITH

Here was a clear case where God was calling on His people to act in faith even *before* they could see how the provision would arrive. Stepping into the Jordan River while the waters were still flowing, not to mention while carrying the holiest and most sacred object in the history of the Hebrew people, was nothing if not an act of total obedience to God's call.

> **STEPPING INTO THE JORDAN RIVER WHILE THE WATERS WERE STILL FLOWING WAS AN ACT OF TOTAL OBEDIENCE TO GOD'S CALL.**

I was running out of time with every passing day because I needed to shoot while we still had winter weather. The screenplay called for snowmobile chase scenes, snow scenes, even a scene in a fishing shanty on a frozen lake. Winter was not a negotiable factor. And winter, even in Northern Michigan, can be unpredictable. I was hoping to begin filming no later than February 1 in order to have confidence that nature would cooperate with our shooting schedule.

The other thing we were fighting was that it really had to be *this* winter. We had a cast and crew of over ninety people, but there was *one* person who would likely not be available again, and that was the one cast member I had to have—Jed. So while some people were recommending we wait yet another year before moving into production, in my mind waiting wasn't an option.

So the question was, when could I pull the trigger and officially green-light the film? When should I actually put in motion the plan that would commit a lot of money and require many people to lock in their schedules? When should I book hotel rooms, crew, and equipment rentals? How was I supposed to live between the tension of Jesus' call to count the cost before building the tower, and Joshua's call to step into the raging waters of the Jordan *before* seeing the waters held back?

This was the inner conflict of my soul in December 2009. We were finally getting some money in. We had gathered nearly half of our budget in investments, and we were planning on taking advantage of a program in our state called the Michigan Film Incentive. With the erosion of auto jobs in our state, and in an effort to diversify our economy, our state was offering financial incentives to companies who would shoot films and spend money in Michigan locations using Michigan crews and talent. I was planning to do both, so we applied for the program and were approved. Those monies helped ease the risk of our investors.

But we still had a long ways to go before I could confidently commit to a production schedule. I wrestled with how to be obedient and wise in this situation. How could I be trusting in the Lord for provision while at the same time not behaving like the foolish man who started building his tower without the funds to complete it?

> **I WRESTLED WITH HOW TO BE OBEDIENT AND WISE IN THIS SITUATION.**

I think that might be right where God wants us to live—totally dependent on Him, while also fully utilizing our own gifts and talents. God's provision for His people in the days of the exodus from Egypt was always just enough for the day at hand, never more and never less. He sent them manna for the day, and they were not to store away any for the next day. That way when the next day came, His people were right back in a place of dependency on Him, back in a posture of expectant prayer and sincere thankfulness. That way we don't forget that it is really all about His blessing and not about our own doing. I finally came to the decision that I was just going to have to be faithful to both Scriptures.

> *For which of you, wanting to build a tower, doesn't first sit down and calculate the cost to see if he has enough to complete it?* (Luke 14:28 HCSB)

I noticed that in this passage Jesus didn't say that the builder had to necessarily *have* the entire pile of bricks or every last dollar in the bank. He says you have to calculate the cost and see if there is enough to complete the project. Well, we *had* calculated the cost; we knew precisely what it was going to take. We also knew we didn't have it all yet, but sometimes God does call us to step out in faith. So with faith and confidence in God alone we launched the film. *The Frontier Boys* got the green light.

Things had to happen quickly if we were going to be in full production by February. The script needed to be broken down into a shot list and storyboard; the shot list had to be strip-boarded into a shooting sequence; locations and lodging had to be secured; and I needed to hire a cast and a crew.

But things began moving quickly, and God provided at every turn. We didn't start filming by February 1; it actually turned out to be February 20 instead. But that just led to another set of "God help us" circumstances. I believe that had it not been for my Jed's obedient ear, his willingness to hear and act on the call of God, the film would not have happened. God asked Jed to do something crazy, to drop out of school and risk his scholarship. But it was God doing the asking, and like all the kids in the ARC groups had learned, whatever God says to do, you do.

> **BUT IT WAS GOD DOING THE ASKING—AND WHATEVER GOD SAYS TO DO, YOU DO.**

God was now leading me and teaching me through my son and his faith and obedience. I remembered again the verse,

> *Train up a child in the way he should go, and when he is old he will not depart from it* (Proverbs 22:6 NKJV).

We called Jed's college and explained our situation. We told the Director of Financial Aid that Jed had a rare opportunity to play a starring role in a feature film. Since Jed had already accumulated enough credits to be a semester ahead of his class, and since he had proven himself to be a good student and a strong covenant group leader in his dorm, we asked if they would consider holding his scholarship for him until the following fall. The Director of Financial Aid was wonderful; she knew a lot about the movie business. Her dad was a producer and her mom was an actress. She said yes.

The waters were slowing down above us.

JED'S SIDE OF THE STORY

By the end of November in my sophomore year of college, we were about 99 percent sure that we were not going to make this film. We had nothing secured except a bunch of people who didn't want to give us their money. But even though the movie didn't seem to be happening, I was becoming convinced that life was about to look different for me.

My freshman year at Point Loma was incredibly good—it was exactly where I knew I was supposed to be. And my sophomore year was also really good, but it wasn't quite as homey. I don't know how else to describe it except to say that I didn't sense that I was absolutely where I needed to be. Since I already felt like I was a little bit out of place at school that year, the email about seeking God's direction regarding the film made me really excited. I still wanted to serve the Lord more than anything, and I started getting ideas of what I might do with the time surrounding movie making.

There was a place in Kansas City that I had heard really good things about called the International House of Prayer (IHOP), and my friends Herb and Sarah (who are brother and sister) happened to be living there at the time. My thought was that this would be a great opportunity to go be in Kansas City with them, be discipled by them, spend some time at the house of prayer, shoot a movie for a month, and then see where the Lord took me after that. I spent a lot of time praying about it, and the more I did, the more confirmed I felt.

> **I SPENT A LOT OF TIME PRAYING ABOUT IT, AND THE MORE I DID, THE MORE CONFIRMED I FELT.**

In the time between initially talking about making the movie and coming to the conclusion that it wasn't actually going to be possible, I called Sarah in Kansas City. "I might be leaving school next semester to film a movie," I told her, and before I even said anything about visiting Kansas, she jumped in and said, "You should come live with us for the rest of the semester!"

The only problem, as aforementioned, was that now it was almost the end of the semester and it didn't look like the movie was going to happen. But somewhere along the line, I had decided in my heart and mind that I was going to drop out of school and go to Kansas City, where the Lord seemed to be leading me—film or no film.

My parents came out for Thanksgiving, and around a table by the bay, sitting with my girlfriend, sister, parents, and my friend Ryan, I broke the news. It was certainly met with a little bit of resistance—possibly a few tears and a few phrases like, "Honestly, think through what you're actually doing right now." But I was pretty set. I was totally fine with saying that my life was in the hands of the Lord, and I would give up financial support if that was what it took. I was going to go where He was sending me.

> **I WAS TOTALLY FINE WITH SAYING THAT MY LIFE WAS IN THE HANDS OF THE LORD.**

So we continued to talk, and I eventually got my parents' support. I had a couple of very difficult conversations with grandparents and other people who questioned my decision, but ultimately I was given at least the understanding that whether I stayed or left, my family would be with me.

I learned shortly thereafter that in my conviction to leave school, a new faith or passion was ignited in my father to pursue the production of *The Frontier Boys*—against all rational odds. So I left school and went to Kansas City, and then I went to Michigan and shot a movie.

One thing that's certain is that all of this is just a testimony to the Lord getting done what He wants to get done and doing things in people faithfully. I didn't handle the next semester perfectly, or even the next year. Kansas City was good, but the lack of structure and discipline for me revealed a lack of structure and discipline in me. I didn't use my time at IHOP nearly as well as I would have liked.

All that summer and even at school the first semester back, I was really lax. In a lot of ways, I just kind of went with the flow of things and didn't pursue anything more deeply or diligently. At IHOP, I prayed and read Scripture, but it was less exciting for me, and I didn't engage it with my heart the way I had before. When I went back to school, I took classes just for the sake of taking classes, and suddenly assignments for reading Scripture became the ones that I didn't seem to finish. Before, I had been taking every single opportunity I had to read and grow in the knowledge of the Word of God; now I wasn't even completing assigned reading passages. Even service toward people, which I had hungered for before, started becoming less of a priority for me.

So I think it's fair to say that in a lot of ways I was failing to grasp what the Lord had offered me—the opportunity and the time to know Him and to prepare. But I find myself now, a year later, at a place where I know the significance of the Word of God, and it's not a flimsy thing based on emotions, but it is the Word of God, which is our life. And the Lord has held me and has created in me a depth somehow of those things—maybe that I wouldn't have understood had I not lost the excitement and emotion I had for a time. And if nothing else, it resulted in a product—*The Frontier Boys* film—which I really believe was by Him and for Him and is filled with His Spirit.

> **I'VE LEARNED THAT THE ONLY OPTION IS TO SERVE HIM, AND THE ONLY THING THAT YOU'LL FIND FROM HIM IS FAITHFULNESS.**

If I've learned nothing else through the experience, it's that God is absolutely God. I've learned that the only option is to serve Him, and the only thing that you'll find from Him is faithfulness. God wanted to grow me, so He made it happen. God wanted to make a movie, so He made it happen.

If we are faithless, He remains faithful; He cannot deny Himself (2 Timothy 2:13 NKJV).

PRACTICING PRINCIPLES

Principle #6: God's timing is always perfect.

Are you willing to step out in faith—even when the future is uncertain? How hard is it for you to rely totally on God? When faith is all you have, is that enough? Have you taught your children how faithful God is and will always be?

CHAPTER 7
PARTNERSHIP

Principle #7: Embrace the shift from parent to partner.

The shooting schedule for *The Frontier Boys* was tough. It was a winter story, and I wanted to shoot much of it at night. I wanted a look and feel that captured the essence of the north and revealed it in its gray and blustery late-winter honesty. There were no scenes calling for bright sunny days. Night schedules, especially when they alternate with day schedules, throw one's body for a loop. And night shooting in the snow and freezing cold is enough to make anybody question why he or she ever wanted to be in the film business.

Every outdoor middle-of-the-night scene in a movie has to be lit, and when you're shooting on location, that means generators, cables, lifts, massive lights, flags and filters, and a lot of tough guys to set it all up and tear it all down. Towable diesel generators have to be located far enough away from the set to keep the noise down for the audio in the scene. That means heavy electrical cables need to be run for hundreds of feet, usually in triplicate. Massive HMI lights have to be lifted high into the sky to simulate moonlight.

The sheer volume of cables, distribution boxes, stingers, and cable guards running all over the place is daunting.

> **NO MATTER HOW GOOD YOUR BOOTS ARE, IF YOU'RE STANDING IN THE SNOW ALL NIGHT LONG, YOUR TOES WILL FREEZE.**

The guys who take care of all of that stuff are called the G&E crew—grip and electric. Our G&E crew was a mixture of guys working below their normal rates and guys working for no rates. They are the hardest working guys in the business, and on our set they were a fantastic team. In cold temperatures those heavy power cables get stiff, and so do one's fingers. No matter how good your boots are, if you're standing in the snow all night long, your toes will freeze. In every scene actors must repeat their action and dialogue multiple times, and each time we change the angle of the camera the entire lighting setup needs to change. To do a reverse shot of a dialogue usually means the whole company has to pick up and pivot 180 degrees. It takes time.

Because we were starting late in February we knew it was imperative that we front-load the shooting schedule as much as possible with all the snow and outdoors scenes. So we began with the most technically challenging scene of the entire film: the snowmobile chase. And just to make it more fun, we set the chase at night.

ON SNOWMOBILES AT NIGHT

Snowmobiles move really fast, and they fly across terrain that can be crazy, bumpy, and unpredictable. This can make cinematography a challenge. Our director of photography, Bryan Papierski, along with the help of best boy Matt Lowing, invented a floating camera tray system that mounted on the back of a snowmobile.

We called it the *Snow Cam*. Our Snow Cam absorbed some of the shock and sway that happens when you are flying along at fifty miles an hour on bumpy uneven snow. The cameraman sat backwards to operate the rig, and his driver tried to maintain constant speed and minimal bounciness. It was a challenging task.

The action sequence we were filming consisted of a chase scene where two "good guy" snowmobiles were trying to get away from one "bad guy" snowmobile. The good guy snowmobiles held two riders each, while the bad guy was a single rider. The chase started at a barn, raced down a path in the woods, turned down a snowy back road, proceeded through the farm country, more woods, a steep mountainside, an ice rink, and a rural road. All in the dark.

About halfway through the chase, the good guys split up, and the bad guy pursues one and lets the other go. With only two snowmobiles left in the scene the climax of the chase happens when the lead snowmobile, with the two good guys on board, runs through a stop sign just in front of a speeding semi truck that comes roaring down the icy road. The bad guy snowmobile is cut off by the truck and has no choice but to hit the ditch and wipe out his machine to narrowly avoid a broadside collision. Did I mention the whole thing takes place at night? You can imagine how quickly a speeding snowmobile can drive in and out of all the nicely lit area you have painstakingly set up.

> **DID I MENTION THE WHOLE THING TAKES PLACE AT NIGHT?**

We hauled around a giant 12K HMI light mounted on a forty-foot Genie Lift. A light this size is about as big as a heavy duty washing machine—the kind you can put a triple load in—and it's about as heavy. Our lighting director was Dean Horn from Grand Rapids, Michigan—one of the most professional and easygoing guys you could ever work with. Dean and his crew patiently set up, pulled down, and set up again that 12K time after time, running hundreds of feet of cable and making each scene look fantastic. One guy, Condor Jim we called him, had the job of sitting forty feet in the air in the bucket along with the 12K light. He sat up in that bucket because if we needed the light to be pivoted one way or another, we didn't want to wait half an hour for the light to move down and then back up again. Condor Jim needed to tend the light. That meant that Jim would sit up in that bucket all night long. He wrapped himself in blankets, did his job, and didn't complain. Later on, the producers started asking one another who had hired Condor Jim? Turned out, no one had. He just showed up on set one day and started working. I'm sure glad he came.

We used stunt drivers for the snowmobiles, but we needed close-ups of our main actors driving the snowmobiles as well. We discovered that it was virtually impossible to get usable close-ups of faces while they were actually racing around on the snow. The vibrations were just too great. So we mounted the snowmobiles on a process trailer and hauled it around the woods behind a pickup truck. The flat bed process trailer was big enough to hold a snowmobile, a generator, a full bank of lights, and a set of pipe safety rails. The actor sat on the snowmobile while the Director of Photography and the First Assistant Cameraman rode on the trailer and belted themselves to the rails. Someone from the art department stood behind the camera and tossed potato flakes into the air to simulate snow.

I sat in the cab of the truck watching the monitor and talking to the actor and the cameraman on the walkie-talkie. It was a bit warmer in that cab at 4 a.m. than it was for those guys outside on the trailer. Being the director has its perks.

We drove up and down the snowy county roads in the middle of the night, our process trailer lit up like a low-flying UFO. The actors pretended to be driving in a frantic high-speed chase scene. We were actually doing about twenty-five miles per hour. We had to shoot in short but intense bursts of action. The pickup driver would honk twice before he began moving, then I'd call "Roll camera," the DP would answer, "Rolling," and then once the shot was settled I'd yell, "Action!" The actor would start pretend-driving, the potato flakes would start flying, and we'd shoot for about thirty seconds or so and I'd yell, "Cut." Then we'd stop the truck, pull over, I'd run back and give a few notes, we'd change lenses or actors, and do it again. Sounds simple enough, but everything takes longer when it's five degrees Fahrenheit. It requires hours and hours of painstaking production work to film what will turn out to be nothing but quick flashes of action in the final edit.

> **SOUNDS SIMPLE ENOUGH, BUT EVERYTHING TAKES LONGER WHEN IT'S FIVE DEGREES FAHRENHEIT.**

We typically wrapped for the night at about 6 a.m. and packed up and went back to the hotel for a quick meal and some sleep. I was staying in a house separate from the rest of the cast and crew. I needed a place that was quiet where I could work. I only allowed two or three hours for sleep on those days because by 9 a.m. I needed to be up preparing storyboards and shot lists for the next day's production.

MOVIEMAKING ON A SHOESTRING

Tight budgets do have consequences. One of them was that I didn't have as many "above the line" personnel as I would have liked. Some key positions weren't even filled when we began production. When the First Assistant Director showed up on the day before production and acknowledged that he hadn't bothered to read the script yet, we cut him loose on the spot. That meant week one was shot without a first AD. When the new first AD finally arrived he helped me move things along at a more rapid pace. He brought a loud voice of authority that was much needed. But he hadn't had the luxury of living with the script for nine weeks and, as such, he wasn't able to manage or generate the daily shot list as comprehensively as we would have liked. That meant I had to anticipate every detail—every prop, setup, cutaway, transition, and angle—in order to be sure we were covered for the upcoming day. I couldn't take the risk that we might inadvertently skip filming an important shot or, even more importantly, that we might run out of time or money before we had the entire story in the can.

> **IT WAS LIVING IN A PRESSURE COOKER FOR A MONTH.**

It was living in a pressure cooker for a month, but I truly felt the support of many of my friends who were praying for my health and focus. The good news was that when we had to make adjustments, if we had to shave scenes or choose alternate locations, I could quickly approve the changes. I was the writer, the producer, and the director. It was probably too many hats for me to wear, but it did make for a very efficient chain of decision. On many films if the director needs to make a change in the script, he or she needs to secure various permissions from writers, producers, agents, and executives. We simply didn't have enough time for those kinds of administrative slowdowns.

My primary job was to anticipate how much we could realistically expect to get shot for each day or night of production. There were days where I thought someone was playing a practical joke on me, moving the hands of my watch ahead just to mess with my head. It seemed to me like time was flying at ten times its normal speed—the polar opposite of those days when I was a kid, sitting in the seventh grade classroom, wondering if the second hand had actually stopped moving on the clock on the wall. I had never experienced ten hours blow by as fast as when I had a long list of angles for a scene that I wanted to film. Time just flew by and I had to prioritize and make tough choices every day.

In addition to the logistical and creative challenges that demanded my focused attention, there was a cast and crew of about one hundred people who needed to be fed, transported, organized, motivated, and occasionally counseled. I felt a burden of responsibility for each one of them.

But I had a lot of help. We had production coordinators, art directors, associate producers, assistant directors, assistant producers, a script supervisor, office interns, and many others who were all working hard to keep things moving smoothly and moving forward. The production office generated daily schedules, maps, and sides. They handled logistics, communicated with vendors and locations, and put out lots of little fires.

MY SON, MY PARTNER

Despite the team and the tremendous cooperation coming from the community, the person I leaned on and trusted the most was Jed. I wanted him to live in the hotel so he could mingle with the other actors. I had confidence that with Jed in the mix, the spirit at the hotel would remain on task and upbeat. I trusted that Jed would represent me well and that he would model everything we were trying to do by honoring God with the film. That's the kind of trust any father would want to have in any son.

> **I PRAYED THAT OUR WORK TOGETHER WOULD HONOR GOD.**

I wasn't naïve. I never expected that every single person working on the film would share everything I believed, and I certainly didn't require every person in the crew to sign a religious or creedal statement. I did, however, expect our leadership team to treat every person in the cast and crew with the love of Jesus, and I prayed that our work together would honor God. I also asked the cast and crew to be respectful to the townspeople and locations we encountered every day.

But I needed someone to pray with me and help me figure out the twists and turns that the modifications in the script were requiring. Who better than Jed to be my prayer partner and script consultant? After all, he was part of the story from the very beginning.

> **THOSE PRAYER TIMES WITH JED WERE THE KEY TO MY ABILITY TO STAY FOCUSED, CALM, AND POSITIVE.**

Every day that Jed was on set I asked him to join me for a moment to pray. Sometimes we ducked out of sight; sometimes we just stepped a few paces away from everybody else. In those moments I felt the favor and peace of God wash over me. Those prayer times were the key to my ability to stay focused, calm, and positive.

Jed's primary job was to act, to give a great performance as one of the lead characters in the film. It was a tall order since he had virtually no acting experience. Greg Myhre, a professional working actor from LA, plays the role of the older brother, Mike Fencett, in the movie. Greg is a great talent, and he was extra helpful to Jed on the set.

Timothy Lofing plays the lead role of Brent Fencett in the film. Jed and Tim's characters are best friends whose relationship goes through a time of testing. Timothy is a professional actor from New York City who had been studying his craft for years, working with some of the best acting coaches in Manhattan. I was a little nervous that Tim's experience and Jed's inexperience would be revealed in the scenes that the two of them play together. But Tim was consistently helpful to Jed. He turned in a tremendous performance himself, and I credit him with helping Jed deliver a terrific performance that was consistent, believable, and powerful.

> **AS WE WERE MAKING THE FILM MY ROLE IN JED'S LIFE WAS TAKING THE SUBTLE TURN FROM PARENT TO PARTNER.**

So we worked together as director and actor, as father and son. I gave him notes on his performances, and he gave me the support I needed in the most stressful times. As we were making the film, my role in Jed's life was taking the subtle turn from parent to partner. We were partners making a feature film. We were partners in prayer, partners in support, and partners in the work itself. I still get to carry the moniker of "Dad" with Jed, but he became more than just "son."

JED'S SIDE OF THE STORY

It was strange for me to be one of the actors in the film, not so much because acting was so hard as far as sweat and blood is concerned, but because it was largely less sweaty and less bloody than the other jobs around. I was forced not to run on set. I was not allowed to do my own stunts because, if I somehow got injured and couldn't work, that would shut production down entirely. I wasn't allowed to touch any of the lights or any of the equipment, not because they couldn't use help, but because I didn't know what I was doing, and if I got burned on my hands or face, I might not look the same as I had in previous scenes.

So the way to do my job effectively was usually to just sit patiently and quietly behind the scenes. Sometimes I would communicate with my dad and voice my opinion about directing stuff, but for the most part, my job was to sit and witness people working significantly harder than I was working and then to get pampered much more than those harder-working people.

> **SO THE WAY TO DO MY JOB EFFECTIVELY WAS USUALLY TO JUST SIT PATIENTLY AND QUIETLY BEHIND THE SCENES.**

I had a pretty good relationship with the production assistants. Two of them, Troy and Tony, were friends from my school. I'd played hockey with Tony growing up and had spent a lot of time hanging out with Troy. We were very similar in a lot of ways, and all of a sudden we were in a position where I got to sit in a warm indoor place and their job was to bring me hot chocolate. Then they got to stand outside holding cold metal pipes for ten hours—in the below-freezing weather—at night. This was awkward for me.

I like to be the one who works the hardest and who serves others as best I can—the one who gets hot chocolate for them. But in this setting I was expected to do otherwise. It was, in a strange way, humbling because again I was forced to learn that what I do and what I have is simply a gift given. But I also learned that there needed to be different gifts, or different jobs, given to different people for anything to work. So I sat and watched, paid attention, and tried not to neglect the people who were doing the grunt work and actually making the film happen. But then, I was making the film happen, too. Without any one of us, there wouldn't be a film.

> **I LEARNED THAT THERE NEEDED TO BE DIFFERENT GIFTS, OR DIFFERENT JOBS, GIVEN TO DIFFERENT PEOPLE FOR ANYTHING TO WORK.**

My dad had another (yet similar) perspective on all of this. He seemed to be even more aware than I was that this opportunity really was given to us, not of our own doing, but as a gift given to and received by us. The fact that we had a crew, equipment, and creativity was a gift. But unlike me—who for the most part got as much sleep as I needed and was able to stay warm and to sit back until I was told what to do—Dad's more central, more spotlighted role on set was one that kept him in the cold just as long as everyone else. He only slept about two or three hours a night, not only for the month and a half of shooting, but also for the month before and after that. He was the hardest working of the working servants.

The role that I played in that space was one that left me humbled and thankful. And when you're humbled and thankful, you try and do the best job you can so that those who you're legitimately grateful for might be served well—even if all you can give is a simple prayer, a simple hug, a simple invitation to the table that you're eating at, or a simple word.

PRACTICING PRINCIPLES

Principle #7: Embrace the shift from parent to partner.

Are you looking forward to the shift in your relationship with your children, or are you intimidated or afraid of the change in your role? Have you enjoyed the shift or are you resisting the adjustment? Why?

CHAPTER 8
BEHIND THE SCENES

Principle #8: Good art imitates life.

Mick Jagger once said, "You can't always get what you want." I wanted a helicopter for some aerials. I couldn't get it—but we did get a small plane that worked pretty well. I wanted two primary cameras for three solid weeks. I couldn't afford it—but we did add a second and even a third camera when we really needed them. I wanted a Techno-Crane and a SteadiCam rig for every day on set. Nope—but we did have a Fisher dolly, and we brought in a Jimi-Jib and Steadi-cam for the most important scenes.

Time after time stuff I thought was going to be a stumbling block or disappointment was turned, by God's grace, into a blessing. One such stumbling block came a mere five days before we began shooting. We had secured an agreement from the actor Stephen Baldwin to play the role of Kevin Bracken, Jed's father. Stephen Baldwin is a well-known actor, famous for his role in *The Untouchables*, among others, and his presence was important to bring a level of credibility to our film. The problem was that we couldn't afford to hire Screen Actors Guild actors for our film. SAG rules stipulate that if one actor in the film is SAG, then you must pay every speaking role the SAG minimums. For us, with almost fifty speaking parts, union requirements would have added over $180,000 of additional expenses that we simply didn't have. We had to do the film as a non-SAG film. Stephen Baldwin found out at the last minute that he couldn't pay an exemption fee and act in the film, as he had been hoping to do. He learned that if he went ahead and acted in the film he would likely lose his SAG card, and that would be a disaster for his career. He felt bad, we felt bad—but there was no way he could honor his commitment to the film. Bummer.

But like so many things along this ride, a disappointment turned into a blessing. A day or two later I got a call from the country singer Big Kenny. We had sent Big Kenny a script earlier and now he was calling to say he'd read it and he liked it. He told me he reads more than thirty scripts each year, and this was the best one he'd seen. He told me he could see the care that had been put into the pages, and it looked like it had really been tweaked, revised, and perfected. I guess that's one benefit to sitting on a script for four years before it makes it to production!

Big Kenny signed on, and from the moment he arrived on the set, he was fantastic. As a member of the country band duo Big & Rich, Big Kenny is well known to millions of his fans. They performed at a Super Bowl! And because he wasn't known as an actor he wasn't a member of the Screen Actors Guild. We could use him! Big Kenny had the potential to raise the interest of a whole lot of people in the country music world that we might otherwise never have had access to. And to top it off, his performance is wonderful. I think Big Kenny gets his stage name not because he is tall, but rather because he is a truly big personality—totally fun and full of life. God is good indeed.

> **WE FOUND MORE THAN THAT; WE KEPT FINDING PEOPLE WHO HAD ACTUALLY LIVED OUT THE STORIES OF THE CHARACTERS THEY WERE PLAYING.**

Stories like that were repeated throughout much of the casting process. I desperately wanted to find talented and believable actors who could embrace the characters on the page and bring them to life. But we found more than that; we kept finding people who had actually lived out the stories of the characters they were playing. Let me share a few examples.

TAYLOR DEROO—T.J. LEWIS

Taylor DeRoo was a high school junior and star basketball player for the Holland High Dutch. During a preseason basketball tournament at Northview High School in Grand Rapids, Michigan, Taylor collapsed on the court and suffered a cardiac arrest. According to the paramedics on the scene, he literally died right there on the floor. He was shocked twice with an Automatic External Defibrillator (AED) and rushed to the hospital. The AED had been installed in that particular gymnasium only one week earlier.

Taylor was in serious trouble. He was shocked three more times in the ambulance on the way to the hospital. That is a lot of shocking. He survived between twenty and thirty minutes basically without oxygen in his bloodstream. When he arrived at the hospital, there was swelling in the brain and Taylor was unconscious. Even if he did survive, the chances of severe brain damage were nearly certain.

His family was told to prepare for the worst, so they began to pray. For three days Taylor underwent a variety of treatments, and his body temperature was dropped to 91 degrees. He was put into an induced coma. Nobody knew if he would live or die or, if he did live, what his functional ability would be. And then, according to his doctors and according to his family, a miracle happened. His high school basketball coach came to visit him and barged in with his big voice booming, "Hey DeRoo...." Taylor's eyes shot open.

Here's how it was described in *The Holland Sentinel*:

> On Sunday his family got a positive response after asking many people to pray.
>
> "Taylor opened his eyes on command and also squeezed the nurse's hand...Thank you, thank you, thank you Great God!"[1]

At first Taylor's short-term memory was shaky. He had no idea why he was in a hospital, and his first response upon returning to consciousness was to get angry with his mom for putting him in this "nursing home." He wanted to get back on the court. But there was a little problem—short-term memory loss includes muscle memory. He couldn't even remember how to tie his shoes. But God was working. The first time his doctor saw him out of his bed, Taylor was not only walking down the hall, but he also was dribbling a basketball. The doctor only had one thing to say, "God is good."

"GOD IS GOOD."

Fox Sports Detroit did a television story about Taylor and aired it during the state high school basketball finals. The host, Trevor Thompson, asked Taylor if he believed in miracles. A big smile filled Taylor's face.

"I have to," he said confidently.

Amazingly, Taylor not only made a full recovery, but he even returned to the basketball court later that same season. Doctors implanted an internal cardiac defibrillator (ICD) in his heart, and with that device he was cleared to play. He regained his full physical and mental capacities.

As I was searching for an actor to play the role of T.J. Lewis, I had a very specific type of guy in mind. For one thing, he had to be a legitimate basketball player. I am bothered when movies pass off actors who never played the game and ask us to believe they are superstars. It never works. I played basketball, and I can tell—as can any former player—if the guy is a poser in about three steps and two dribbles. T.J. Lewis was supposed to be the best basketball player the town had seen in decades. He simply had to be a real player.

Second, the T.J. Lewis in the script is a young man of impeccable character. He is quiet and strong, and he has deep and real faith. He is easy to like, and he gets along well with his father and his sister. I needed an actor who could embody all these qualities.

And one more thing. T.J. gets shot early in the movie. He spends most of the film lying in a coma with a breathing tube in his mouth. Now, I didn't expect to find an actor with real life experience in that arena—but I did. Taylor DeRoo is all those things. His real life story is of God bringing him back to life and health through answered prayer and miraculous intervention. If anybody sees our film and says that miracle stuff is just fantasy and wishful thinking, then I just point to Taylor DeRoo. It actually happened to him.

I went to visit Taylor at his home right during the middle of his senior basketball season. He was performing at an all-conference level and had started every game for Holland High School. I was invited into the living room, and I entered with my DVD movie trailer and a poster in my hand.

"Taylor, I want you to be in this movie," I started with. I showed him the movie trailer and told him all about the project. I told him how my friend Pam had thought of him and had stopped by my office to suggest we consider him for the part. Pam didn't even know Taylor; she just felt led to suggest him to me.

I knew this was a long shot. Principal photography for the movie was in Charlevoix, four hours north of Holland, and Taylor

141

was in the middle of high school basketball season. Plus, he had to go to school. I didn't really know how to make this work, but I pledged to him that, if he were willing, I would do everything possible to not interfere with his basketball schedule or his school schedule. He agreed to think about it and to pray about it—but I could tell he wasn't sure about the idea. I didn't blame him.

The DeRoo family themselves have quite a story, and it's kind of funny how I first got to know them. Sara and Doug DeRoo began adopting kids in 1989. They started with a beautiful little girl of Korean descent and then added another girl and then four boys. The last five are all black. Sara and Doug are white. By 2003, the DeRoo family had six kids, ages six through twelve. It was a lively household to say the least. But then, in January of 2003, Doug DeRoo was killed in a car accident only a few blocks from his home. Sara was left on her own with a house full of kids and no husband or father in the mix.

During that time, the DeRoo family lived in a neighborhood just behind the neighborhood where our family lived. A couple of years later we happened to meet the family, thanks to our dogs. We had a young beagle puppy named Jackson (foreshadowing his namesake in the film) who liked to run away from home and go exploring. Beagles do this. His expeditions often ended up at the DeRoo household, where Jackson cavorted with their young female beagle, Penny.

> **A COUPLE OF YEARS LATER WE HAPPENED TO MEET THE FAMILY, THANKS TO OUR DOGS.**

We had to trudge over there to fetch our dog so many times that we got to know the DeRoos well. My wife and Sara discovered that they had been at Hope College at the same time, and they developed a good friendship. Jed was a classmate of one of the DeRoo girls, and the two of them shared a love for animals—beagles in particular. The kids devised a beagle-breeding program that culminated with Jackson and Penny copulating in our living room to the cheers and laughter of all six of the DeRoo kids, both of our kids, and me. Penny went on to give birth to seven beagle puppies, and once again, all the kids were present for the event. The experience makes us feel related to the DeRoos, like we're beagle-in-laws.

A few years later Sara met a man named Jamie, a widower with six kids of his own. They fell in love and married, thus creating a twelve-child blended family of blended race. They are the Brady Bunch on steroids, and they are amazing people. It is into that backdrop that I dropped in on Taylor and asked him to consider the role in the film.

Taylor finally agreed, and we arranged for shuttles to bring him back and forth from Holland to Charlevoix on many late night/early morning trips. The chauffeur was usually Judy, my wife and our executive producer. Judy often would leave the set in Charlevoix around 4 a.m. with Taylor asleep in the backseat. She would drive through the night and drop him off at school in Holland just before eight in the morning.

It was quite a sacrifice for everyone involved, and it took the cooperation of his family and his coaches. But he never missed any basketball games, and he only missed one practice. We scheduled most of his scenes for Saturdays and Sundays, and we secretly prayed that the Holland High Dutch would not go *too* far in the state tournament that year. Taylor graduated high school and moved on to play college basketball at Dominican University in Chicago. He is quite a dude.

EARTHQUAKE KELLEY—REVEREND LEWIS

T.J.'s father in the film is the character known as Reverend Lewis. He is one of the pillars of strength and godly masculinity that I wanted to model in the film. Reverend Lewis is an ex-football player, an outgoing pastor, and a bit of a trailblazer. He is a black pastor leading a mostly white northern church because in the Body of Christ there are no racial divisions. Reverend Lewis is a minister, but he is also human. He is capable of losing his temper and thrashing out in his darkest hour.

I was looking for an actor to play Reverend Lewis, and to be honest, I wanted Denzel. Denzel Washington is one of my favorite actors. He has played good guys and bad guys, and when I watch Denzel, I see the very qualities I envisioned for Reverend Lewis. I always think Denzel plays his characters spot on, full of integrity and strength. I've heard that he is a man of faith as well, so I was hopeful. I sent a script to his agent. His agent sent it back unopened. Things with Denzel didn't look too promising.

My problem was that when I auditioned other actors, I wasn't really auditioning them. I was comparing them to Denzel. That is a lousy way to audition, and if you do that, you will never be satisfied. Several strong candidates auditioned for the part, but I couldn't make up my mind. So I waited. And waited.

> **I DECIDED TO TRUST HER. IF I COULDN'T BE SURE, THEN I WOULD TRUST SOMEONE WHO WAS.**

It was down to two days before I needed Reverend Lewis on the set and I had rejected every single actor who had auditioned for the role. Finally one of our casting associates, Carolyn Hoover, came up to me and said she was sure—she had a very strong feeling—that Earthquake Kelley was right for the role. She believed that it was God's will. That's a pretty strong endorsement. It took real conviction on her part to come out with so strong a statement. I decided to trust her. If I couldn't be sure, then I would trust someone who was.

Earthquake was excited about the role and was on a plane within a few hours of getting the news. At least, he tried to get on a plane. Bishop Curtis (Earthquake) Kelley is a huge man. A former Olympic heavyweight boxer, he is now a preacher and evangelist who lives in Los Angeles. His own story is one of a young man who was as angry and rebellious as a young man can be. His father was a practitioner of voodoo, and Earthquake learned witchcraft concepts as a child. He was into drugs by age four and cocaine by age ten. But he gave his life to the Lord in the early '70s and found an outlet in boxing. His boxing career is where he earned the nickname Earthquake. He hit so hard, I am told, that heavyweights like Mike Tyson and Leon Spinks refused to even spar with him.

> **HE POUNDS HIS FIST INTO HIS HAND AND SHOUTS, "WHO WOULD SHOOT AT A CHILD, WHO!"**

But there is more to Earthquake. He started a ministry with his family and began sharing his testimony and the redemptive power of God. His son Scott was part of the ministry, and one day in 1998 his son was shot at point-blank range and killed. The very people Earthquake had been trying to help through his ministry were the very people who took the life of his son. It is a story so reminiscent of Jesus.

In the film, Reverend Lewis experiences the anguish of a father when he learns his son has been shot. He is deeply saddened, but he also has within him a hidden rage at the senseless brutality of someone who would point a gun out of a car and shoot at a group of innocent kids. In one scene Reverend Lewis is found in the middle of the night, passing time in the hospital waiting room. His anger gets the best of him, and he pounds his fist into his hand and shouts, "Who would shoot at a child, who!" Jed's father, Kevin Bracken, comes over to console him, but Reverend Lewis is out of control.

When we shot that scene, Earthquake Kelley turned in one of the most powerful moments in the film, one of the most powerful moments I've seen in any film. He pounds his fist and loses himself entirely in the moment. Big Kenny comes over to be a brother and try and console him, but Earthquake is full of rage. He tosses Big Kenny around like a rag doll. The scene is so moving because we know that Earthquake knows that rage firsthand. It is an amazing moment on the screen, and I am deeply honored to have him play the role. We almost never got him to the set at all. Earthquake left Los Angeles in plenty of time to make it to Northern Michigan for a Monday shoot schedule, but one airplane after another cancelled their service. Seven consecutive airlines didn't fly that day because either the pilot didn't show up or there was mechanical failure or who knows what. I fly a lot, and I know that air travel can be unpredictable at best. But I've never run into a string of seven straight flights that wouldn't leave the ground. We began to wonder if there were forces larger than ourselves trying to prevent Earthquake from making it to the set.

We were shooting scenes in a coffee shop in the Northern Michigan town of Mancelona. I had looked all over the region to find the right location for this coffee shop and was delighted with the location. Mancelona has a little extra charm because of Ernest Hemingway's references in the Nick Adams stories. Our little coffee bar had a cool northern vibe; it looked like we had designed it from scratch. We had dressed the set, secured the releases, and were scheduled to film there for just one day.

We also only had actor Ted Swartz for one day. Ted was in town to play the role of Bucky the barista. Bucky is a fun character; he banters and jokes with the boys and is an important part of their history. Ted Swartz is a longtime friend of mine and one of the best actors I know. His enterprise, Ted & Company, writes and performs incredible original works of theater all over the country. He travels a lot, and his schedule was extremely tight. It was generous of him to agree to be in the film at all—especially for the peanuts we were paying. But he came for one day. He had a show on Tuesday, and he needed to fly out that morning. Thus, there was stress on the set all day Monday when Earthquake did not arrive. We needed to shoot scenes where Earthquake and Bucky interact. There were scenes where we were to see Bucky in the background while Earthquake talked with the boys.

This was my fault. If I had decided sooner, then this last-minute travel wouldn't have been a problem. We had to try and knock off some of the scenes, even if Earthquake wasn't on location. So we created a stand-in for him and shot over the shoulder angles. We dressed up my buddy Bruce in the outfit that costume supervisor, Elizabeth Flores, had selected for Earthquake to wear in the scene. Bruce is a big guy, and the reverse shots worked really well. But we needed Earthquake. It was midnight when he finally arrived. Everyone on set cheered when he came in, and we quickly threw him into wardrobe and makeup. It was late, but all the actors were still on set. I was pushing. We needed to get this done, and Ted really had to leave soon. But when Earthquake came on set and we rolled the cameras, we realized we had a major problem. The man was totally, completely, unsalvageably exhausted. He had been traveling for forty-two consecutive hours. There was nothing in the tank.

> **THERE COMES A POINT WHERE THE MIND IS WILLING, BUT THE FLESH IS WEAK. WE WERE PAST THAT POINT.**

There comes a point where the mind is willing, but the flesh is weak. We were past that point. We were at "the mind is asleep and the flesh needs to pass out." I had no choice; we had to call it for the night and push the schedule.

The next day, we returned and shot all of Earthquake's scenes. He was awake, and he was splendid. Ted was gone, so we dressed our Second Assistant Director, Tony Narwocki, in Ted's clothes and used the back of his shoulders that day.

Earthquake Kelley proved Carolyn Hoover right. He continues to be a major blessing to me, to the film, and to many of the cast members. His heart is as big as he is. He even gave us our first national exposure for the film when he appeared on TBN and talked about *The Frontier Boys*. They showed the clip on television where he pounds his fist in the hospital, and soon after that, the switchboard at TBN was lighting up like crazy. Everyone wanted to know when the film would be released.

Earthquake embraced the role of Reverend Lewis and brought it to life. Now I've heard he has kept in close contact with Taylor DeRoo. Imagine that: Earthquake Kelley, who lost his son, keeping in contact with Taylor DeRoo, who lost his father. I've heard Earthquake has been like a father figure to him. Once again, good art imitates life.

JED'S SIDE OF THE STORY

My dad started the previous chapter recognizing that you can't always get what you want. Whew. That's a relief. God speaks in Isaiah,

> *As the heavens are higher than the earth, so are my ways higher than your ways and my thoughts than your thoughts* (Isaiah 55:9).

And in Romans it says,

> *For who has known the mind of the Lord? Or who has been His counselor? Or who has ever first given to Him, and has to be repaid? For from Him and through Him and to Him are all things. To Him be the glory forever. Amen* (Romans 11:34-36 HCSB).

One of my more frequently recurring and wretched sins is my tendency to rebel against the wisdom of God by propping up my own wisdom. Romans also says,

> *For by the grace given me I say to every one of you: Do not think of yourself more highly than you ought, but rather think of yourself with sober judgment, in accordance with the faith God has distributed to each of you* (Romans 12:3 TNIV).

In short, I think more highly of myself than I ought. I tend to overestimate my own understanding, my grasp of truth, my perfect fairness and judgment, my ability to reason, my perfectly weaved systematic thinking with perfect recognition of its own incompleteness. I even recognize my own ability to justify myself under any circumstance.

Since I am able to recognize my downfalls, my laziness, and my apathy in repentance prayers and discussions, I allow myself to be comforted by this self-awareness. It's like I somehow have tried to convince myself that I am the only sane person in the world, the only one who truly sees properly.

I naturally assume that I live life very reasonably, maintaining a sense of control by maintaining confidence in my awareness and ability to judge fairly. In all honesty, although I call Jesus my master, my guide, the one who is in control, I maintain my own self-mastery, reason-led guidance, and self-control through this prideful boasting of my inner vision and perspective.

I often act unlike the faithful blind man in Luke.

As Jesus approached Jericho, a blind man was sitting by the roadside begging. When he heard the crowd going by, he asked what was happening. They told him, "Jesus of Nazareth is passing by." He called out, "Jesus, Son of David, have mercy on me!" Those who led the way rebuked him and told him to be quiet, but he shouted all the more, "Son of David, have mercy on me!" Jesus stopped and ordered the man to be brought to him. When he came near, Jesus asked him, "What do you want me to do for you?" "Lord, I want to see," he replied. Jesus said to him, "Receive your sight; your faith has healed you." Immediately he received his sight and followed Jesus, praising God. When all the people saw it, they also praised God (Luke 18:35-43 TNIV).

Compare that with the Pharisee described in Luke:

The Pharisee stood up and prayed: "God, I thank you that I am not like other men—robbers, evildoers, adulterers—or even like this tax collector. I fast twice a week and give a tenth of all I get." But the tax collector stood at a distance. He would not even look up to heaven, but beat his breast and said, "God, have mercy on me, a sinner." I tell you that this man, rather than the other, went home justified before God. For everyone who exalts himself will be humbled, and he who humbles himself will be exalted (Luke 18:11-14 TNIV).

You can see the contrasts so clearly. The blind man and the tax collector recognized their own complete helplessness, and they cried out with fervent desperation to the one who could truly save them. The Pharisee, sensing his own self-accomplishment, didn't cry out to the savior at all. His prayer was more like a little lecture toward God, recounting for the Lord how good he truly was. Jesus sees the heart, and I know which heart I truly desire.

I'm not properly aware of how much God loves us. I long to *feel* it in all of me, with everything in me. If I were to know its depths, I just don't know what I would do.

> I'M CONVINCED JESUS IS THE TRUTH, AND THE HOLY SPIRIT IS QUITE SIMPLY THE SPIRIT, AND WE'RE MEANT TO WORSHIP IN THEM.

I desire to live life in Spirit—to worship in Spirit and in Truth. I'm convinced Jesus is the Truth, and the Holy Spirit is quite simply the Spirit, and we're meant to worship in them. Not that there's really any other way. Who could honestly worship God and offer himself up daily as a living sacrifice to the Lord any other way than through Jesus and the Holy Spirit?

HOW TO FOLLOW?

If someone were to say to me, "Hey, follow Joe there. He really knows what he is doing—you'll do well to learn from that guy," it would be clear to me what to do. I would listen to Joe, let him show me how to do things, watch him, and learn from him. I'd have some questions, and I'd probably take his advice. If I truly desired to follow Joe, even though there would be a learning curve, I would know how to persevere. I'd be an apprentice until I learned the craft. The question, "How is it possible that I might learn from Joe?" would never come up. If I decided to learn from Joe, I would not at all be surprised if Joe gave me a book to read, providing a foundation for our relationship and his teaching.

And if it happened that my apprenticeship was not only to learn a specific topic or trade craft, but was even more basic than that—so that I might become like Joe in every way—then I guess I wouldn't be surprised to learn that Joe had written the guidebook himself.

> **SO THEN WHY DOES IT SEEM SO DIFFICULT TO GRASP WHAT IT MEANS TO FOLLOW JESUS—TO LIVE BY THE SPIRIT, TO WORSHIP IN SPIRIT AND TRUTH?**

So then why does it seem so difficult to grasp what it means to follow Jesus—to live by the Spirit, to worship in Spirit and Truth? For me, I suspect the answer is that I tend to forget that Jesus is alive or that the Holy Spirit is, quite frankly, real. The other tendency, for me, is to sometimes think that the Spirit might be real for other people, but not for me.

Without wasting words, I'll address the issue.

Is Jesus really alive?

Yes. More so than you or me, or anyone else ever.

Like, actually alive?

Yes, eating and breathing.

Is the Holy Spirit *real*?

You bet. But don't think you can control Him.

The wind blows wherever it pleases. You hear its sound, but you cannot tell where it comes from or where it is going. So it is with everyone born of the Spirit (John 3:8).

Is the Holy Spirit like any other teacher or leader?

No, He is the *only* teacher and leader. In fact, in Matthew 23:9-10, Jesus tells His disciples,

And do not call anyone on earth "father," for you have one Father, and he is in heaven. Nor are you to be called "teacher," for you have one Teacher, the Christ.

Not only is He not like any other, but He also is so far above that we mustn't even call others by the same title.

Is the Holy Spirit for me?

He is for you even more than you are for yourself.

Which of you fathers, if your son asks for a fish, will give him a snake instead? Or if he asks for an egg, will give him a scorpion? If you then, though you are evil, know how to give good gifts to your children, how much more will your Father in heaven give the Holy Spirit to those who ask him! (Luke 11:11-13)

I had a lead role in a movie, was pampered on the set by the crew, and now see my face on big screens, posters, and DVD covers, and I ask myself—am I concerned with this world, coveting its praise but fearing its rejection? This is the dangerous trap of any form of success, of any kind of worldly recognition. Will I again begin to rely on myself, on my own cognitive abilities, on my own sense of moral superiority, secretly believing that I'm the only really sane one? Or maybe I'll carve out a little compromise—I'll determine my steps, but they will largely resemble God's ways. I have to be in control, but I will let my spiritually-enlightened intellect guide me.

Straight into death.

Jesus said,

Don't fear those who kill the body but are not able to kill the soul; rather, fear Him who is able to destroy both soul and body in hell. Aren't two sparrows sold for a penny? Yet not one of them falls to the ground without your Father's consent. But even the hairs of your head have all been counted. So don't be afraid therefore; you are worth more than many sparrows (Matthew 10:28-31 HCSB).

As much as it's true that Jesus is alive, it is true that if you lose your life for His sake, you will find it. This is my choice. I can learn to live in the way God wants me to live by and for and through the Holy Spirit. Thank God you can't always get what you want. And thank God that He does get what He wants. And thank God He wants you alive.

PRACTICING PRINCIPLES

Principle #8: Good art imitates life.

When God brings others into your life, do you appreciate them for who they are and accept their special qualities? Do you allow the Holy Spirit to guide you in your thoughts and actions toward others? How do others view you and your relationships with God and your children?

NOTE

1. Jeremy Gonsior, "Teen still in hospital after Friday collapse – Holland High basketball player remains in serious condition," *The Holland Sentinel*, Nov. 30, 2008, last update Dec. 1, 2008, http://www.hollandsentinel.com/news/x776465378/Teen-still-in-hospital-after-Friday-collapse-Holland-High-basketball-player-remains-in-serious-condition.

CHAPTER 9
MAKE IT REAL

Principle #9: With God, we always have a future.

All great adventures must come to an end, including filming movies and raising kids. For the cast and crew of *The Frontier Boys*, the end came with the night we shot a large and furious fire, kind of like an apocalypse. For weeks we were known around Northern Michigan as "that movie that wants to burn down the historic house." Well, I guess it's true. We did want to burn down the historic house. But I must clarify: the house was going to be demolished anyway. We just thought, *If she has to go, why not send her out in a blaze of glory?*

The script of *The Frontier Boys* called for two major pyrotechnic scenes. The first one called for a burning barn; the second involved a Molotov cocktail that is thrown through a window, causing a house fire.

A burning barn is a powerful image, and I really wanted it for the film. In the screenplay, the bad guys use a backwoods barn as their secret lab and headquarters. They are making crystal meth in the barn. In Michigan, backwoods barns are sometimes being used for crystal methamphetamine production because the cooking process is so odorous. A barn that sits a long way off the road in a rural or isolated area is an inviting setting for an illegal drug manufacturing operation.

In the story, Frank Snelling is the least self-controlled of all the would-be gang members, and he, through his foolishness, draws unwanted attention to the barn. Before long the police are sniffing around the place. The gang locks down and goes dark, but the leader, Sean, knows the cops will eventually be back. He orders his boys to leave everything behind and to move out immediately. Later when the Frontier Boys return with the police to the scene of the crime, the barn and any evidence it may have contained are consumed in a giant inferno.

In order to shoot this scene, I needed a barn to burn, and it couldn't be the barn we actually shot our gang scenes in. That barn was owned by Ridge Point Community Church in Holland, and they graciously let us use the barn; they even let us cut a second floor window in the barn. But they weren't very keen on us burning it down. Understandable.

We searched all over Michigan for a barn we could actually burn, ideally one near some woods. After much looking, we found just such a place. The barn owners, after some prayer and reflection, agreed to give us permission to film their barn being burned down. Their barn was old and they were going to have to have it razed anyway. This seemed to be a way for them to get rid of the dangerous barn and preserve its memory forever. It was a very generous gesture on their part.

> **THE BARN OWNERS, AFTER SOME PRAYER AND REFLECTION, AGREED TO GIVE US PERMISSION TO FILM THEIR BARN BEING BURNED DOWN.**

I scouted the location and mapped out the camera angles. We were going to shoot through the woods, and we would come to the scene after the barn was well along in the burning process. That way any visual differences between this barn and the Ridge Point barn would be minimized.

But our barn burning never happened. The conditions in Charlevoix County turned dry, and the Fire Commissioner ruled that it was too risky to ignite a big fire like that so near the woods. I was really bumming because we had worked so hard to find a barn, and the scene really was crucial to the story.

We did, however, have permission to burn the house. I talked with our Graphic Artist Trevor Lee, and we came up with a solution. Trevor was confident that if we took plate images of the Ridge Point barn in Holland he could create a 3D-model of the barn and then burn it graphically. He planned to use the real flame from the house fire to composite together a realistic-looking barn burning.

So we shot green screen shots of the four boys pretending to walk up, as if looking at a burning barn. We shot them from the front and from the back, and we lit them with fire-simulating flicker lights. The composite barn burning shots turned out even more convincing than my original plan because the images of the barn on fire were images of the actual barn we had seen earlier in the film. Once again, what seemed at the time to be a major disappointment ended up being a major blessing.

Ironically, eight months after we completed shooting, the Ridge Point barn actually did burn to the ground! I couldn't believe it. Nobody who sees the film is going to believe that we had nothing to do with it. But I'm telling you—we didn't.

BURNING DOWN THE HOUSE

Our final night of principal photography was the night we really were going to shoot the burning of the historic Charlevoix house. But before we could actually light the place up, we needed to shoot some scenes inside the house. In the story, Frank Snelling runs up to the window of the house and throws a lit Molotov cocktail through it. The fuel ignites as it scatters across the wooden floors of the old house, and the innocent family that was sitting in the house is terrified.

We had to dress the interior of the house before we burned it down. Our Art Director, Nancy Terryn, along with the Set Designers, Julie Dugger and Nancy Janosi, went to work finding furniture, curtains, wall hangings, and plants. They painted the walls, installed safety glass in the window, and ordered sugar glass bottles for the Molotov cocktail. When we shot the flaming bottle crashing through the window, our Director of Photography, Bryan Papierski, and the First Assistant Cameraman, Stephen Taylor-Wehr, were actually in the house, and the real flames spread incredibly quickly. Our camera crew was surrounded by gas-mask wearing firefighters who were prepared to quickly put out the fire once we had the shots we needed.

Even though we knew what to expect, our camera team still came out of the house coughing. It's amazing how quickly the smoke gets so thick you can't breathe unless you drop to the floor. I've always heard that was the case; that night I saw it: stop, drop, and roll! After we finished with the interior scenes, we took a break for lunch. It was midnight.

The house burning was big news and a crowd of people gathered on the sidewalks to watch. The 100-year-old house had stood vacant for twelve years. Earlier the Charlevoix Historical Society had hoped to convert it into a museum or something, but no one had come forth with the money for such a project. Repair estimates ran as high as a million dollars, and in the end the City Council voted to raze the house to make room for more downtown parking. The Historical Society was on hand that night because they intended to remove the doors and windows and anything else that had historical value just before we actually burned the house.

Unfortunately, as we went to lunch they went to work. We hadn't yet shot any of the exterior shots of the house, but when we came back at 1 a.m. to begin filming, we discovered that the house had been stripped. The doors were gone, the windows were gone—the place looked like an abandoned shell, not the nice cozy home of an innocent family that we needed to shoot. It's always something. It took some time to find where they had taken the front door and so we could put it back in place. We couldn't put the windows back in, so we resorted to stretching gaff tape across the windows in order to simulate window grilles. It looked okay, but I don't linger for too long on the exterior shot in the final edit.

There were a number of dialogue scenes that I needed to shoot before we really let the house burn, so the Charlevoix Fire Department brought flash pans that they could ignite and extinguish multiple times inside the house. They worked great. We started the fire, shot some dialogue in the street, called cut, and put the fire out inside the house. Then we changed angles and did it again. We pulled this off four or five times before we were ready for the grand finale.

> **BY 5 A.M. WE WERE FINALLY READY FOR THE LAST SCENE.**

By 5 a.m. we were finally ready for the last scene. I gave the Fire Department the go-ahead, and they set the whole house ablaze. The crowd of onlookers, which had been over a hundred earlier in the night, was down to the last hearty dozen or so, but oh my, what a show they got. That old house lit up like the whole thing was made of newspaper. It just raged. We had three cameras shooting the action, but the fire was so spectacular, I temporarily forgot what I was doing. I was as spellbound by the action as the onlookers.

The footage that we shot of that old house burning was some of the most stunning fire footage I have ever seen. We enjoyed tremendous cooperation from the Charlevoix City Fire Department, from the EMT crew and ambulance, from the local Sheriff and Police Departments, from the State Police, and from the City Council. The historic old house, which had stood at 108 Park for 100 years, took no more than forty-five minutes to burn completely to the ground. By 6 a.m. she was nothing but burning embers, suitable for roasting marshmallows.

"IT'S A WRAP"

And that was it. It was a wrap. It marked the end of the most intense month of my life. At the end I stood shoulder to shoulder with Jed as the behind-the-scenes crew interviewed us. We stood in front of the ashes of the old house and reflected on how so many things in life are here today and unexpectedly gone tomorrow.

> **ABSENT OF OUR HOPE IN CHRIST, LIFE WOULD BE A DREADFULLY SCARY PROPOSITION.**

Absent of our hope in Christ, life would be a dreadfully scary proposition. Houses that hold 100 years of memories can be erased from the face of the earth in less than an hour. So can lives.

Parenting can feel like that too. For eighteen years or so, you arrange your schedule, your conversations, your hobbies, and the bulk of your attention on the comings and goings of your children. And then they are gone. They move away; they go to college; they get married. In some cases, they die.

As I stood by the last embers of that fire with my arm around my nineteen-year-old son, I felt the satisfaction of a job done well and the promise of great things to come. And that's how it is with God. No matter how old we are or what station of life we are in, with God we can always look forward. We can remember our past with gratitude, we can appreciate how His work in our lives has brought us where we are, and we can always look forward with sincere anticipation. God is always before us.

> **NO MATTER HOW OLD WE ARE OR WHAT STATION OF LIFE WE ARE IN, WITH GOD WE CAN ALWAYS LOOK FORWARD.**

Jed had just finished starring in his first movie. The shoot was over. But he had the future on his mind. After we wrapped, he packed his things and headed back out to California. He hadn't seen his girlfriend, Brittany, for a long while, and he had something to give her. It was a diamond that had belonged to my grandmother, in a gold band that had belonged to my wife, alongside an engagement ring for her finger. He needed to have a little talk with her father first.

So to all you who are fathers or mothers or aunts or uncles or brothers or sisters or mentors or guardians, know this: Your love will change the world through the children God has put under your care. It's how He made things work.

For from Him and through Him and to Him are all things. To Him be the glory forever. Amen (Romans 11:36 HCSB).

JED'S SIDE OF THE STORY

I am twenty-one years old now, and I am engaged. Brittany—the best-looking girl in all of California—said yes. We have about a year until we are going to get married, but I don't imagine we will wait too terribly long before having children of our own—God willing. I am already looking forward to being a father myself.

I've heard my dad speak about his experience of having and raising children. He has admitted that the responsibility was, at first especially, daunting. The thought of his that sticks with me is, "How in the world am I supposed to know how to do this? What qualifications do I have for raising a child? I've never done this before."

What do I offer, from the perspective of a son, as the greatest advice to fathers? Live by the Spirit and pray that your son does as well. Relinquish ownership over your son. Give God what is His. There is no greater gift than God Himself.

> **GUIDE YOUR SON BY WORSHIPING THE ONE WHO GAVE HIM TO YOU.**

This is not apathy. This doesn't look like leaving. But it is humbling. You just end up meeting God. Guide your son by worshiping the One who gave him to you. Respond in gratitude by giving back all that God has given to you—namely, your life and your son. I certainly don't feel like my dad loved me any less because he has entrusted me to his God. Quite the opposite.

And although I am yet to have children, I am already forming in my mind a picture of what it might be like to have a child with the woman I love, to bring into the world a life that is utterly beyond my own ability to create and yet completely thrust into my care. I'm starting to imagine the feelings of inadequacy. It seems to me that children are gifts given that we are not fully qualified to bear responsibility for because they are never truly ours alone anyway. They are a gift, and they are a reflection of God because they remind us of how much He loves each of us. My dad has said that he never knew he really had the capacity for unconditional love until my older sister was born. That baby, lying on his tummy in the late 1980s, taught him that he could love even more perfectly than he thought he could. That is God's nature within us.

> **GOD IS NOT ONLY THE GIVER OF GOOD GIFTS, BUT HE ALSO IS THE ULTIMATE GIFT.**

Here is the end: God is not only the giver of good gifts, but He also is the ultimate gift. God gave my mother and father the gifts of two children. I had absolutely no say in the matter. God gave each of us His own Son and access to His own Spirit. And Jesus has given Himself as the complete answer and gift to the world. Jesus said,

I am the way, the truth, and the life… (John 14:6 HCSB).

From Him, to Him, and in Him are all things. If this is true of all things, it is certainly true of life between fathers and sons. Receive gratefully from God, walk with Him, and find yourself fully in Him, as He has desired to place Himself in you.

PRACTICING PRINCIPLES

Principle #9: With God, we always have a future.

Have you faced challenges and tribulations with a sincere hope and a special knowing that God is in your future—that He is more than willing and able to bring you through every situation? Have you conveyed this hope and knowing to your children? Have you publicly and privately exhibited your confidence in God for your future?

CHAPTER 10
A THOUSAND GENERATIONS

*Principle #10: Learn to reflect the Father
as a father.*

You have an incredible opportunity to make an indelible stamp on the future of the world simply by raising a son who becomes a man of God. What it requires is prayer and intention on your part. Jed and I have shared our story with you in hopes that through our honesty and experience you will find the path with your son that leads you both closer to God.

And when you think about it, you are the first and most practical image your son has of God. Jesus calls the Father "Abba"—Daddy. You mimic some of the characteristics of God when you show generous love, loving discipline, guidance and counsel, and a welcoming spirit.

GENEROUS LOVE

One reason to show generous love to our children with our resources, with our affection, and with our time is because God has shown generous love to us.

For God so loved the world that He gave His only begotten Son, that whoever believes in Him should not perish but have everlasting life (John 3:16 NKJV).

Generous love is a *choice* you make when you have children. You become a better man than you were before as you become more selfless and generous. You *discover* that you have within you the capacity to love unconditionally. It's crazy, but you discover that you actually love your children before they have done anything to earn that love. In this way you are becoming more like the Father. When you recognize that you have the innate capacity for this kind of love, it comes like a shock!

> **WHEN YOU RECOGNIZE THAT YOU HAVE THE INNATE CAPACITY FOR THIS KIND OF LOVE, IT COMES LIKE A SHOCK!**

Becoming a parent was the reality check that finally began to teach me that my life was not all about me. In truth, my marriage should have done that. But learning how to be truly selfless in marriage is still sometimes a conditional process for me. This is not because of Judy; she has been an incredible wife and partner. The fault lies in my selfish and sinful nature.

Parenting, however, proved to be different right from the start.

We love Him because He first loved us (1 John 4:19 NKJV).

By having a child I suddenly had the opportunity to mimic the nature and character of God by discovering the potential for unconditional love in myself! This was radical. I remember lying on the couch with my one-month-old daughter asleep on my chest. I had the sudden and vivid realization that I loved this little girl, and that there was nothing that she could do to change or earn that. Wow! I never thought I had it in me. The same was true for my son, and the same is true to this day.

> **HE LOVES US FIRST, AND WE IN TURN LEARN TO LOVE HIM BACK.**

God gave me a glimpse of His own nature when I discovered that I had something in me that reflected His heart. He loves us because we are His children. He loves us first, and we in turn learn to love Him back. That is how it worked with my kids. Our love came first, and then later, that love is returned.

LOVING DISCIPLINE

Generous or unconditional love does not preclude the need for discipline. As you are a reflection of the Father you are also a reflection of God's willingness to discipline those He loves. As your children grow, you will become acutely aware of the rebellious and sinful nature that they will naturally exhibit. Taming that nature and nurturing that nature will not happen through your neglect or passivity.

> *Blessed is the man whom God corrects: so do not despise the discipline of the Almighty* (Job 5:17).

The nature of your discipline is an important matter for you and your spouse to come to full agreement on. Talk it out. When our kids were very young, under age three, they were essentially too young to fully understand my compelling arguments regarding appropriate behavioral concepts. Especially before they spoke English. Therefore, on rare occasions, I would use corporal discipline—one quick swat on the bottom. This was never done in anger, but it was an appropriate deterrent for behaviors like running into the street, beating your sister with a stick, or screaming so hard your face turned purple. Beyond age three or so, however, I was finished with corporal discipline. Beyond that young age I believed corporal punishment would produce more rebellion than obedience.

As our kids gained a bit of maturity, we were able to reason with them, to explain the options. By age five corporal discipline was completely replaced by expectation and consequence. We wanted to foster a true desire in our kids to behave in God-honoring ways, not merely a mandatory compulsion to do so.

> **WE WANTED TO FOSTER A TRUE DESIRE IN OUR KIDS TO BEHAVE IN GOD-HONORING WAYS, NOT MERELY A MANDATORY COMPULSION TO DO SO.**

When our daughter graduated and went to college we gave her a car. It was an old car, one we had owned for a while, but for her it was—and still is—a great way to get around San Diego. So naturally kid number two, Jed, wondered if a car was coming his way when he graduated. The answer was: not necessarily. For one thing I've never been an adherent to one-size-fits-all parenting. For another, I didn't really have another spare car lying around. Nevertheless I made Jed a deal. There were two simple chores around the house that I wanted him to be responsible for: trash every Monday, and scooping the dog poop. I told Jed if he could handle those two chores for the entire school year, he'd get a car when he graduated. Used car. I also told Jed this would be the only time I would bring up the deal, and he would either pass or fail. I wasn't going to remind, supervise, cajole, or coax.

Unfortunately he didn't make it two weeks. I never mentioned it again; I simply resumed taking out the garbage when necessary and cleaning up the dog's fecal deposits. At graduation time Jed got a bike. Granted, it was a really cool and very fast bike, and it was a great present for the hard work he had done in high school; but he didn't get a car, and he knew exactly why.

I tell that story because I think that reward and consequence are a natural part of life, and we do our kids no great favors when we try to insulate them from that reality. The reality is that God is also a God of wrath and judgment.

> *For if God did not spare angels when they sinned, but sent them to hell, putting them into gloomy dungeons to be held for judgment; if he did not spare the ancient world when he brought the flood on its ungodly people, but protected Noah, a preacher of righteousness, and seven others; if he condemned the cities of Sodom and Gomorrah by burning them to ashes, and made them an example of what is going to happen to the ungodly; and if he rescued Lot, a righteous man, who was distressed by the filthy lives of lawless men (for that righteous man, living among them day after day, was tormented in his righteous soul by the lawless deeds he saw and heard)—if this is so, then the Lord knows how to rescue the godly from trials and to hold the unrighteous for the day of judgment, while continuing their punishment* (2 Peter 2:4-9).

Just as our unconditional love for our kids is a reflection of the character of God, so is the need and desire to discipline them as they grow up. To be strategic, prayerful, and consistent regarding this issue is incredibly important.

GUIDANCE AND COUNSEL

Kids don't naturally know how to do stuff. Neither do we. The story of God's people in the world is the story of God continually calling and training them to live in the way He wanted them to live. Think about the Hebrews forty years in the wilderness. God gave guidance and counsel to His people for forty years because they did not know how to represent Him to the world. They were in training.

> *Remember how the Lord your God led you all the way in the wilderness these forty years, to humble and test you in order to know what was in your heart, whether or not you would keep his commands* (Deuteronomy 8:2 TNIV).

Your kids are no better. You want them to represent your family name in the world? It's going to take guidance and counsel. It will be a challenge. You must teach them how to consider the other guy, how to be generous, how to be thoughtful. You must practice this together as a family, and you must model it for them as well.

> **DO NOT NEGLECT THE TIME IT TAKES TO TEACH YOUR SON HOW TO DO THE THINGS YOU KNOW HOW TO DO.**

Do not neglect the time it takes to teach your son how to do the things you know how to do. I couldn't teach my son how to fix a car, but I could teach him how to hit a golf ball. Unfortunately for him, that is not as practical a skill as fixing the car. But what really matters in the exchange is the exchange itself, not necessarily the skill. If you know how to frame-in a house, drive a tractor, fix a sink, clean a deer, throw a knuckleball, shoot a camera, play the guitar, or even run a business—by all means, teach your boy what you know. Don't force him to like it. Don't expect that it will be his passion just because it is yours, but take the time to share with him what you've learned.

When you share guidance and counsel with your son, you are mimicking a characteristic of God in the life of your son, and that matters even more than the transfer of a particular skill or ability.

A WELCOMING SPIRIT

Finally, you are a representation of God to your son as you demonstrate a welcoming spirit. God is always available; we never have to make an appointment on His schedule. He has sent the Holy Spirit to come and dwell within us. It doesn't get any more welcoming than that.

> **HE HAS SENT THE HOLY SPIRIT TO COME AND DWELL WITHIN US.**

This is the final of my four characteristics that I challenge you to follow because this one speaks most closely to your attitude. A welcoming spirit says to your son, "I like you, I value you, I enjoy your presence, I am enthusiastic about you." Of course, your son's behavior will not always inspire such emotions in you. Of course there are times he is going to drive you almost crazy. But you are, after all, mimicking the nature of God here. Remember the story of the prodigal son? The younger of two sons demands his inheritance, leaves the family estate, heads off to a distant country, and squanders everything in wild living. This boy's behavior was disrespectful, harmful, wasteful, and sinful before God. Nevertheless, here is the response of the father on the day the boy returns.

> *But while he was still a long way off, his father saw him and was filled with compassion for him; he ran to his son, threw his arms around him and kissed him"* (Luke 15:20b).

That is a welcoming spirit. Regardless of your natural personality, your son needs to know that your door is always open, that his phone calls will always be answered, and that he always has access to his father. As you do this you are, again, mimicking a characteristic of God in his life. You are demonstrating that you care. Remember, God has said to you,

> *Cast all your anxiety on him because he cares for you* (1 Peter 5:7).

RAISING A MODERN FRONTIER BOY

I said at the outset that a modern frontier boy is one who is ready and equipped to take on the unknown challenges of the future with courage and faith. As I write this closing chapter I am sitting in a little cabin along the Pacific, one day before my son graduates college summa cum laude, and one month before he marries his college sweetheart, Brittany. I am so happy for him and proud of him. I thank God that I got to play the role of Director in the film we did together, and in many respects play the role of director in his young life. It was a co-directorship, certainly, with my wife—but like any director I have to accept a certain responsibility for the ultimate outcome and success of the project.

The real measure of the success in parenting isn't measured by the man my son becomes as much as it is by the man *I've* become through the process. Being a father is important, of course, in the lives of your kids. But it is even more important in how it has shaped and developed you as a man. You have been given a charge, a responsibility, and a ministry. When you allow God to use you for each of those callings, you become more a man of God than you knew you could be.

I hope this book has been of some help and encouragement to you as you play the role of director in the life of your son or sons. It is your calling to guide them in such a way that they will become real men whose lives and characters are forged in the Word of God, who themselves become great husbands and fathers for the next generations.

> **IT IS YOUR CALLING TO GUIDE THEM IN SUCH A WAY THAT THEY WILL BECOME REAL MEN WHOSE LIVES AND CHARACTERS ARE FORGED IN THE WORD OF GOD, WHO THEMSELVES BECOME GREAT HUSBANDS AND FATHERS FOR THE NEXT GENERATIONS.**

Being a director is a demanding yet rewarding job. It's always a bittersweet moment for me when we finally nail the last shot, and I call out, "It's a wrap." That's how I feel at the end of this road of parenthood, standing looking backward over twenty years or so of raising infants to toddlers, tweenagers to teenagers, college students to married young adults. It's a wrap. I already miss the way being a father challenged me to model things that God wanted for me to model.

And while the focus of this book has been with an eye toward developing the unique nature inherent in masculinity and the specific role you have as a father of sons, I must acknowledge that raising a daughter who has blossomed into a beautiful woman of God is as satisfying and gratifying as any achievement of my life.

> **STRIVE TO BE THE RARE MAN OF GOD WHO PASSES ALONG A GENERATIONAL BLESSING.**

So as you begin or continue your journey as father, I encourage you to deepen your own walk with the Lord, strengthen the way you honor and love your wife, and defy the family-destroying odds of our modern culture. Strive to be the rare man of God who passes along a generational blessing, for according to the Bible the victory you attain by raising a modern frontier boy will have benefits for a thousand generations.

> *For I, the Lord your God, am a jealous God, punishing the children for the sin of the fathers to the third and fourth generation of those who hate me, but showing love to a thousand generations of those who love me and keep my commandments* (Deuteronomy 5:9b-10).

Can you think of anything more worthy of your complete devotion and commitment? May God walk with you, dads, as you head off into the frontier of parenthood.

PRACTICING PRINCIPLES

Principle #10: Learn to reflect the Father as a father.

Do you consistently mimic the characteristics of God by showing generous love, loving discipline, guidance and counsel, and a welcoming spirit to your children? Are you willing to deepen your walk with the Lord, strengthen the way you honor and love your wife, and defy the family-destroying odds of our modern culture? Have you allowed God to use you to raise your children to trust, love, and obey Him? If so, you have become more a man of God than you knew you could be.

Jed's graduation day.

Jordyn and Jed, sister and brother.

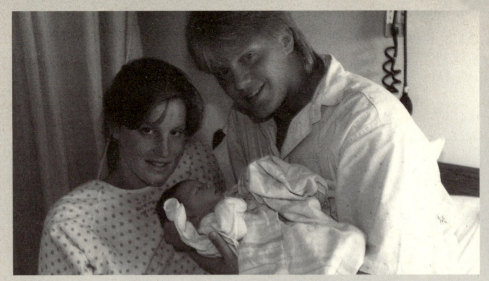

Who can be prepared for fatherhood? Not me.

Sledding is fun... and free!

Jed playing.

Dad coaching, Jed playing.

By high school – Dad wasn't coaching anymore.

The Spring Break anti-beach vacation.

John has filmed all over the world.

Making up stories on the chair lift.

At this point in Jed's life, I think he heard me, but he wasn't really listening.

Jed entered his senior year of high school expecting to become a doctor or engineer.

Jed's freshman year at Point Loma was incredibly good.

A group of friends pray for Jed immediately after his baptism in the Pacific Ocean.

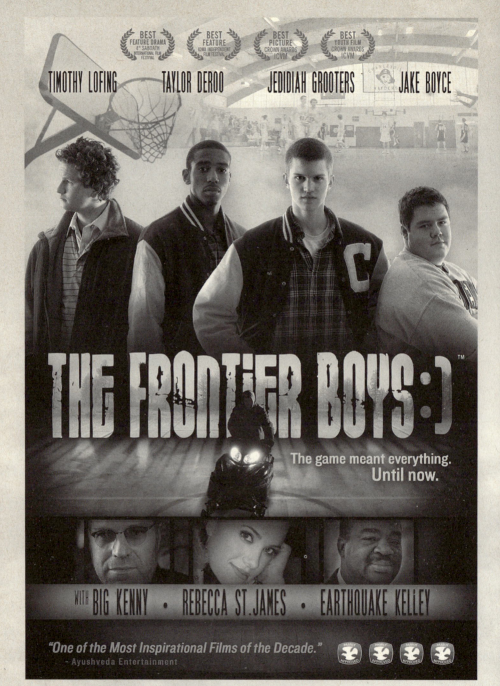

Scenes from *The Frontier Boys*.

The "Snow Cam."

40 foot crane shot for closing scene.

Earthquake Kelly

Taylor DeRoo

Big Kenny

Last night of production!

John watches Jed on the monitor.

Rebecca St. James with The Frontier Boys posing like supermodels.

Brittany & Jed

June 16, 2012

By the time you read this, the wedding will have come and gone. Brittany Grooters is her new name.

CONTACT INFORMATION

To contact the author, call, write, or find online:

John Grooters

17 W. 6th St.
Holland, MI 49423

616.546.4000 (o)

info@grootersproductions.com

www.johngrooters.com

www.facebook.com/johngrooters

DESTINY IMAGE PUBLISHERS, INC.

"Promoting Inspired Lives."

VISIT OUR NEW SITE HOME AT
WWW.DESTINYIMAGE.COM

FREE SUBSCRIPTION TO DI NEWSLETTER

Receive free unpublished articles by top DI authors, exclusive discounts, and free downloads from our best and newest books.
Visit www.destinyimage.com to subscribe.

Write to: Destiny Image
            P.O. Box 310
            Shippensburg, PA 17257-0310

Call: 1-800-722-6774

Email: orders@destinyimage.com

For a complete list of our titles or to place an order online, visit www.destinyimage.com.

FIND US ON FACEBOOK OR FOLLOW US ON TWITTER.

www.facebook.com/destinyimage
www.twitter.com/destinyimage